Joseph Pulitzer and William Randolph Hearst: The Publishers Who Transformed the Media Industry

By Charles River Editors

Pulitzer

About Charles River Editors

Charles River Editors is a boutique digital publishing company, specializing in bringing history back to life with educational and engaging books on a wide range of topics. Keep up to date with our new and free offerings with this 5 second sign up on our weekly mailing list, and visit Our Kindle Author Page to see other recently published Kindle titles.

We make these books for you and always want to know our readers' opinions, so we encourage you to leave reviews and look forward to publishing new and exciting titles each week.

Introduction

Joseph Pulitzer

"Publicity, publicity, publicity is the greatest moral factor and force in our public life." –
Joseph Pulitzer

Say the name Pulitzer and the minds of many across the world quickly turn to the famous
prizes given for excellence in journalism, literature, and music, but these prizes were named after
a man believed to have been tormented by some of the choices he had made during his life.
Coming to America as a nearly penniless immigrant, he demonstrated that the young nation
could be a land of opportunity, and he earned money and fame largely through hard work. Later,
as the owner of one of the most powerful papers in the country, he seemed to develop an almost
frenzied need to stay on top, no matter the cost. Writing for the *Post-Dispatch* in 1997, Harry
Levins observed that Pulitzer considered journalism "a serious instrument of civilization, yet in
some periods filled his front pages with froth and sensationalism. Sided with the common man,
yet lived like the Gilded Age millionaire he was. Waxed indignant at big business and its profit-
seeking machinations, yet insisted that his own big business turn a tidy profit."

Indeed, in an effort to turn a profit, plenty of his contemporaries believed he went way too far.
In a battle to sell papers, he played a significant role in the burgeoning industry of "yellow
journalism," and following the Spanish-American War, he often struggled to come to terms with

the role he had played in getting America involved in that conflict. As he grew older, he would attempt to step away from that reputation, and in an effort to redeem himself, he bequeathed much of his fortune to organizations that could establish scholarships and even the first school of journalism, teaching future journalists who came after him to do better.

Hearst

"Any man who has the brains to think and the nerve to act for the benefit of the people of the country is considered a radical by those who are content with stagnation and willing to endure disaster." – William Randolph Hearst

When William Randolph Hearst was in his late 50s and at the height of his power, journalist Robert Duffuss observed, "His career is unique in American history, or, for that matter, all history. Compared with him the Bennetts and even the Pulitzers are small…his acquaintances…credit him with personal charm, but do not deny his ruthlessness in business operations. Shopkeepers and his nearest rivals are simply not in his class. Here is success on a dizzying and truly American scale. Here is journalism as large as the Rocky Mountains or the Painted Desert."

However, despite his massive success, and perhaps in large measure because of it, many of Heart's contemporaries depicted him in negative ways. As Duffuss also noted, when it came to the newspaper magnate's reputation, there was "a curious suggestion of lath and plaster about it, and far from being universally honored and admired as other self-made men have been, Mr. Hearst is regarded by multitudes of his fellow citizens with extreme aversion and distrust. Indeed, his career is almost never examined dispassionately and for this reason some of the salient facts about him are worth setting down in a somewhat cold-blooded manner." This was never more apparent than during the release of *Citizen Kane,* a barely veiled biography of Hearst which managed to cut him so deeply that he forbade his papers from making reference to the critically acclaimed classic.

It is only right to keep every positive and negative viewpoint in mind when looking at the life of a man who built his own fortune with money inherited from a father who literally grubbed it out of the ground with his own hands. While the senior Hearst may never have gotten the soil of old California from under his nails, William Randolph would never know what it felt like to live a life of manual labor; instead, he founded his empire on another kind of dirt, that which he was able to dig up and publish about the people, great and small, of his day. He would also stir up a good bit of dirt himself, living a high life with his mistress in California while his wife raised their children and did charitable work back in New York. Eventually, he would go too far, and nearly lose his empire when he backed Adolf Hitler over Franklin D. Roosevelt. By the time he died, it is fair to say that he had seen it all, done it all, bought most of it, and lost much of it. In spite of all this, he left behind an empire that continues to dominate the publishing business to this day.

Joseph Pulitzer and William Randolph Hearst: The Lives and Careers of the Publishers Who Transformed the Media Industry examines how both men forged vast newspaper empires and revolutionized how stories were covered, for better and worse. Along with pictures depicting important people, places, and events, you will learn about Pulitzer and Hearst like never before.

Joseph Pulitzer and William Randolph Hearst: The Lives and Careers of the Publishers Who Transformed the Media Industry

A Start in a New Country

"It is to such men as Abraham Lincoln and Jefferson and Jackson and Franklin, all most lowly born, that we owe most of our greatness as a nation." – Joseph Pulitzer

Joseph Pulitzer, or Pulitzer József as he was known in his native Hungary, was born on April 10, 1847, in Mako, a small town about 125 miles southeast of Budapest. His parents, Elize Berger and Fulop Pulitzer, belonged to a small, tightknit Jewish community in the area. Biographer Don Seitz described the circumstances of his childhood in Hungary: "Commonly described as a 'poor emigrant lad,' who had fled from poverty to better his condition in the New World, Mr. Pulitzer was nothing of the sort, save as his bold venturing brought on its own hardships. His family was one of standing in the community, both father and mother being superior people, having means and education. The mother had great personal beauty and the father much character. … The boy was sent with his oldest brother Louis to a private school and further had the advantage of a special tutor. … The family lived comfortably at Budapest until the death of the father. He had been for some years an invalid, with heart disease. The family fortune, though not exhausted, was impaired to an extent that did not permit permanent idleness on the part of the sons. Early in. 1864, during the excitement over the Schleswig-Holstein question, Joseph Pulitzer applied for a commission in the Austrian Army, where two of his uncles, brothers of his mother, were officers. Weak eyes and an unpromising physique, showing the ill-effects of too rapid growth, deprived him of a cadetship. Determined upon a military career, he found his way to Paris and endeavored to join the celebrated Foreign Legion for service in Mexico…." Unfortunately, "The same weakness that excluded him from the Austrian Army operated here. From Paris, after this disappointment, he made his way to London, hoping to find a place in the British forces for service in India. He was again unsuccessful and, despairing, made a start for home via Hamburg. Here he sought employment as a sailor, but his frail appearance was against him and he found no berth."

That's when Pulitzer's destiny changed. Seitz explained, "At this time Europe swarmed with agents seeking recruits, in the guise of emigrants, for the Union Army. The boy fell into the hands of one of these and was shipped to Boston. Arriving in port, in company with another who had been 'recruited' in this fashion, he decided to collect his own bounty, and slipped over the ship's side at night; being an expert swimmer, he safely reached the American shore some time in August or in September, 1864. The irregularity of his arrival obscures the date. Not caring to linger in Boston, which he had invaded so unceremoniously, he made for New York, then the center of military activity as well as the metropolis of the country."

Once in New York, Pulitzer learned that he could earn $200 (more than $5,500 today) for serving in the Union Army in place of a wealthy man who had been conscripted. This would be in addition to the salary he could expect to receive, so he happily took the money and enlisted in the Lincoln Cavalry on September 30, 1864. Fortunately for the young man, if there was ever a good time to join the Civil War, he picked it, because the war was only a few months from ending.

Pulitzer spent most of his eight months of service with soldiers under the command of "Little Phil" Sheridan, which brought him to small skirmishes throughout Virginia. The assignment also meant Pulitzer would be on hand for Robert E. Lee's surrender at Appomattox Court House in early April 1865.

When Pulitzer arrived in America, he was already fluent in Hungarian, German, and French, but despite his participation in the Civil War, he did not actually master English until he returned to civilian life in 1865. During this period in his life, he lived first for a short time in New York City, and then for a longer period in New Bedford, Massachusetts. New Bedford did not suit him, so he moved back to New York City before deciding to try his luck further west.

When he reached East St. Louis on the cold, wet evening of October 10, 1865, there was just one more obstacle to overcome before he reached his destination. He vividly recalled, "There was no bridge across the Mississippi. Passengers had to cross on a ferry boat for which an extra charge was made. I don't remember how much the charge was, but it made no difference for I had not a cent. … The lights of St. Louis looked like a promised land to me. But how to get across the river was a problem. A ferry boat came into the slip. I edged my way down to the gates, hoping something might turn up to help me. Two deck hands of the ferry boat came to the end of the boat near the gates. I heard them speak in the German language. I ventured to call out to them in German. …one of them came up to the gate and I got to talking with him, finally asking if there was any way I could get aboard and across the river. He said that one of the firemen had quit and they might need a man in his place. He went to the engineer, who came and asked whether I could fire a boiler. I said I could. … He said he would take me and opened the gate, letting me on the boat."

At that moment, Pulitzer had his first encounter with stoking a boiler in a storm, an experience that left him "roasting in front and freezing in the back." He worked all night, and the next day he landed in St. Louis, ready to make his fortune.

St. Louis already had a large German population, but as a recently arriving immigrant with only a basic command of the language, it was inevitable that Pulitzer would have to initially find menial jobs. As it turned out, even he wasn't ready for what was coming his way. The first job Pulitzer could find was caring for a herd of mules, a job that he later called his most trying task. He quipped, "The man who has not cared for sixteen mules does not know what work and troubles are." Pulitzer quit that job after only two days, instead opting to work on the ferry, a job that kept him from starving until he found other work as a stevedore. He then got a job in construction.

One of the first pleasures that Pulitzer discovered when he settled in St. Louis was that the city offered him regular access to books. He often visited the Mercantile Library, where he became friends with the librarian, Udo Brachvogel. The two would remain close for the rest of their lives, and Pulizer would spend most of his free hours there, reading and studying to improve his English. The written word was all important to him, and he was determined to be its master.

An 1870 picture of the St. Louis Mercantile Library

A Start in Politics and Publishing

"I desire to assist in attracting to this profession young men of character and ability, also to help those already engaged in the profession to acquire the highest moral and intellectual training." – Joseph Pulitzer

As he got settled in St. Louis, Pulitzer gradually began to move up in the world, getting a job working for an attorney and then later, through the Deutsche-Gesellschaft (a German-American aid society), as a bookkeeper in a lumber yard. When he did well at that job, he landed work as a surveyor for the Atlantic and Pacific Railroad.

Regardless of how often he switched jobs, Pulitzer spent every minute of his spare time studying in hopes of becoming an American citizen, a task he accomplished in March 1867. He also continued reading to improve his English, and studying to become an attorney, a goal he reached in the same year. He spent the next few months of his life largely in service to other German immigrants, and when he needed a break, he would forsake his evening visits to the library in favor of a less literary venue, usually at a saloon run by German immigrants. There he would drink, though rarely to excess, and play chess with anyone who would join him in a game. In this manner, he soon came to enjoy the regular company of Dr. Emil Preetorius, co-editor of the *Westliche Post*, a local German newspaper. Preetorius introduced Pulitzer to his co-editor, Carl Schurz, a fortuitous connection since Schurz was a former lawyer in Milwaukee who became a general during the Civil War. Schurz would go on to become a luminary in Republican politics and the first German-born naturalized citizen to be elected to the U.S. Senate in 1869.

Preetorius

Schurz

Preetorius and Schurz set Pulitzer's feet on the path of destiny when they hired him as a reporter in 1868, paying him $10 a week. Pulitzer was wildly ambitious, and he immediately set about to learn every job at the paper, from writing his own articles and editorials to setting them in type and running the printing press. The reporters for the English-speaking papers called him Joey because he was so young, but they soon learned that there was no one to mess around with. Writing of Pulitzer at this time, William Fayel, who also worked at the paper, recalled an incident when Pulitzer rushed to cover a story: "I remember his appearance distinctly…In one hand he held a pad of paper, and in the other a pencil. He did not wait for inquiries, but announced that he was the reporter from the Westliche Post, and then he began to ask questions of everybody in sight. I remember to have remarked to my companions that for a beginner he was exasperatingly inquisitive. The manner in which he went to work to dig out the facts, however, showed that he was a born reporter. He was so industrious, indeed, that he became a positive annoyance to others who felt less inclined to work…The consequence was that the city editors of the English papers soon discovered that the Westliche Post often contained news which the other reporters had failed to obtain. Major Gilson was then city editor of the Democrat, and every reporter on that newspaper had occasion to remember an order which he posted on the bulletin-board. …it directed the reporters to give less time to attempts to delude the German reporters and more time to work in competing with them. That ended the efforts to curb the new reporter's activity, and we all soon learned to appreciate and make the most of his extraordinary capacity for news gathering. He was quick, intelligent and enthusiastic, but of all his qualities the most notable was his determination to accomplish whatever he set out to do. … Mr. Pulitzer's chief ambition at that time seemed to be to root out public abuses and expose evildoers. In work of this kind he was particularly indefatigable and absolutely fearless."

One of Pulitzer's early beats was the Missouri Legislature, located in the state capital at Jefferson City. Still young and idealistic, he was shocked by the corruption and graft he found within that seemingly august body. Determined to bring it to light, he began to write one article after another criticizing state legislators, and his words eventually caught the eye of Missouri's Republicans. The Republicans made Pulitzer a delegate to their next convention, and when they found themselves in need of a candidate for the Fifth District in late 1869, they chose Pulitzer.

When he was chosen, Putlizer was months short of being a legal adult, and he had been at the *Post* for less than a year. In fact, he had been in America itself less than five years. While all of this sounds highly unusual, it was a testament to the fact that the district was heavily Democratic, and it was almost universally believed to be unwinnable for any other party. However, none of that deterred Pulitzer, who surprised everyone by immersing himself in the campaign and ultimately winning the seat, in spite of the fact that he was not old enough to serve.

Incredibly, since the voters had ignored his age, the Missouri State Legislature chose to as well, so Pulitzer served in the State House and worked at the *Westliche Post* simultaneously for a time. This strange arrangement eventually put undue stress on the young man, and it led him to make a terrible mistake. Writing of the nearly disastrous event on January 27, 1870, one of Pulitzer's fellow journalists, Wallace Gruelle, explained, "Tonight, about half past 7 o'clock, Mr. Pulitzer shot at and wounded Mr. Augustine in the office of the Schmidt Hotel. It appears that Mr. Pulitzer…had sent an article to the *Westliche Post*, at which Mr. Augustine took offense, and mildly told Mr. Pulitzer that he was a liar. Mr. Pulitzer cautioned Mr. Augustine against using such strong language. Mr. Pulitzer left the hotel and got a pistol and returned and went for Mr. Augustine. Had not his pistol been knocked down, Missouri would have been in mourning this day for a slaughtered loyal son. As it was, only two shots were fired, one of which took effect in Augustine's leg. Augustine struck Pulitzer on the head with a Derringer, or some other kind of pistol, cutting his scalp and ending the battle. Mr. Pulitzer was arrested and gave bond for his appearance before the City Magistrate of Jefferson City."

Two days later, another publication, the *Missouri Democrat*, told readers, "There is great excitement and the act is generally declared one of shameless and murderous intent. The ball was extracted by Drs. Hurtt and Thompson. The St. Louis delegation held a meeting, but took no action, although there was general mortification and no one justified Pulitzer. It will doubtless be brought up in the House to-morrow, as all agree it is a disgrace to St. Louis. The pistol was taken away from Pulitzer by C. C. Cady. It was a Sharp's four-barrelled weapon and two balls were discharged."

Back east, this event might have brought an abrupt end to Pulitzer's fledgling career, but Jefferson City was still considered part of the West in the 1860s, and duels and shootings were not viewed with the horror that they would be just a generation later. Pulitzer was convicted of assault and given a fine, but he ultimately served no jail time.

Pulitzer ran for office again as a Republican in 1870, but this time he lost his seat. Discouraged, he left the Republican Party for an offshoot, the Liberal Republicans, who ran Horace Greeley as a presidential candidate in 1872. The *Westliche Post* supported Greeley, so it was a good fit for Pulitzer, who served as the secretary at the party's national convention. He also spent hundreds of hours campaigning for Greeley, often giving lectures in support of the famous New York editor. Greeley ultimately lost the election and died weeks after it, and Pulitzer became even more disenchanted with Republican politics. In the wake of the election, he joined the Democrats.

With his early stint in politics behind him, Pulitzer returned to journalism and soon had a new opportunity on his hands. Years later, he explained, "When I was only twenty-five, some of the proprietors of the *Westliche Post*, in St. Louis, became nervous, wanted to retire, thought the paper was ruined by the Greeley campaign, and sold me a proprietary interest in that paper on very liberal terms. They thought I was necessary to the paper. They probably would have done the same thing to any other man who worked sixteen hours a day, as I did through that campaign."

As one of the paper's owners, Pulitzer worked harder than ever, throwing himself into uncovering corruption at the highest levels of state government. He also spent a lot of time railing against gambling, a growing problem. Even with English being a fourth language, he quickly became an excellent writer and proved more than capable of captivating readers with dynamic prose. The paper prospered, but his fellow owners again became nervous, fearful that he would eventually decide to leverage them out. Thus, they bought him out for $30,000.

After selling his stake in the *Westliche Post,* Pulitzer was comfortable from a financial standpoint, so he took the time to return to Europe for an extended visit, no doubt anxious to show his family that he had done well for himself in America.

When he returned to America in later 1873, however, he immediately began looking for a new project. He found it by purchasing another German-language newspaper, the *Staats-Zeitung*, during a bankruptcy sale on January 6, 1874. Pulitzer's primary interest in the paper lay in its Associated Press franchise, and he sold it to the *Globe* a day later for $20,000. He made a little more money by selling off the machinery.

Shortly after flipping that paper, Pulitzer returned to the political arena he loved so much, and he served as a delegate to Missouri's Constitutional Convention in 1875. In 1876, he campaigned for the Democratic candidate, Samuel Tilden, ahead of what became one of the country's most controversial elections. Given his writing skills, perhaps it's no surprise that Pulitzer eventually became a good orator, and he came to love oratory. On October 31, 1876, just days before the election, Pulitzer spoke at Cooper Union in New York City, the same venue where Lincoln had given one of his most iconic speeches. Pulitzer told the audience, "I stand here to say that the war is over, and it is time that it should be. When the South was wrong I did not hesitate to enlist against it; but today, when the South is not wrong, but wronged, I do not hesitate to enlist for it. The rebel of today is he who robs the Government; the traitor to the Union is he who tries to make peace and unity impossible. The enemy of the Government is he who disgraces a position of public trust. The Southern people belong to us, and we belong to them. Their interests are our interests; their rights should be our rights; their wrongs should be our wrongs. Their prosperity is our prosperity; their poverty is our poverty. We are one people, one country and one government; and whoever endeavors to array one section against another and endeavors to make the union of all people impossible is a traitor to his country."

It's fair to say that no one who was in touch with the national situation believed that the Election of 1876 was going to go smoothly. It was common knowledge that fraud was rampant across the nation, with both parties pulling out every trick in the book to get their way. People who had been dead for years managed to "vote," while those who were alive were turned away from the polls if they were not deemed worthy of being able to cast a ballot. These were problems that plagued regular elections, so there was little hope that the one held on November 7, 1876 would be any different.

At the end of Election Day, it was clear that Tilden had carried the popular vote. On November 8, the *Galveston Gazette* reported, "Unless there is some radical error in the indication of figures thus far received, the election of Tilden and Hendricks may be claimed with absolute certainly. The total electoral vote is 369, and 185 are required to elect. In Democratic estimation before the election as many as 205 voted were set down to the Tilden column, and 184 in the Hayes column. This made the possibility of Hayes's election depend on his getting the thirty-five votes of New York, not conceded to him, or twenty-one or more votes from other States claimed by the Democrats. Hence New York becomes the chief battle ground towards the close of the canvass, and the loss of that State by the Republicans may be laid to have decided the general result for Tilden. The occasion is one for joy and congratulation beyond the power of words. The good sense and the intelligent patriotism of the American people have once more prevailed. The country is redeemed—the future of this republic is safe."

However, the joy of the editors of the *Galveston Gazette* and other Democratic papers was short lived, because immediately below that story was a last minute addition that stifled everyone's early hopes: "3 A.M.—Northern Republicans concede 184 electoral votes to Tilden, claiming, Florida, Louisiana, Nevada, Oregon and South Carolina as doubtful, any one of which States would secure Tilden's election."

Ben Perley captured the mood of the capital shortly after the election results began to come in, and just how unprecedented the situation was: "Washington was wild with excitement immediately after the Presidential election. The returns received late on Tuesday night indicated the election of Mr. Tilden, and even the Republican newspapers announced on the following morning the result as doubtful. Senator Chandler, who was at New York, was the only confident Republican, and he telegraphed to the Capitol, 'Hayes has one hundred and eighty-five votes and is elected.' He also telegraphed to President Grant recommending the concentration of United States troops at the Southern capitals to insure a fair count. President Grant at once ordered General Sherman to instruct the commanding generals in Louisiana and Florida to be vigilant with the forces at their command to preserve peace and good order, and to see that the proper and legal boards of canvassers were unmolested in the performance of their duties. 'Should there be,' said he, 'any grounds of suspicion of fraudulent count on either side, it should be reported and denounced at once. No man worthy of the office of President should be willing to hold it if counted in or placed there by fraud. Either party can afford to be disappointed by the result. The country cannot afford to have the result tainted by the suspicion of illegal or false returns.'"

Oregon and Nevada were quickly decided for Hayes, giving him 166 electoral votes, but the three Southern States hung in the balance. By this time, there had been so much fraud and intimidation exercised by both parties that there was really no way of knowing what the honest totals were. Intent on making sure that the vote count in South Carolina, Louisiana, and Florida was accurate and untainted by Democratic Party intimidation, the Republicans set up "returning boards" to oversee the recounts of ballots.

Needless to say, the stakes could not have been higher; Hayes needed all 19 electoral votes from those states, while Tilden was only one elector away from the presidency. Perhaps not surprisingly, the results from the returning boards only inflamed the issue when all three states were awarded to Hayes, with the Republican being declared the winner.

Louisiana's unofficial tallies had shown Tilden the winner by some 6,000 votes, but the Republican controlled returning board threw out 15,000 due to allegations of fraud and voter intimidation, giving the state's 8 electoral votes to Hayes. In South Carolina, the same scenario worked itself out, with enough votes being thrown out that the state went for Hayes, along with nullifying the victories of the Democratic gubernatorial candidate and Democratic legislators. In both states, the Democrats set up rival state governments (each with their own governors and legislature) and awarded the state's electoral votes to Tilden.

In Florida, the state that subsequently played a central role in the contested election of 2000, the situation was even more complicated. The first vote tallies showed Hayes the victor by just 43 votes, but a recount had Tilden victorious by 94 votes. The Republican controlled returning board disallowed enough ballots to deliver the state to Hayes by about 1,000 votes, and this action, as it had in Louisiana and South Carolina, had the added effect of overturning the gubernatorial result and awarding the office to the Republican candidate. Further complicating the situation, the Florida Supreme Court threw out these results and awarded the governorship to Democrat George Franklin Drew, who promptly announced that Tilden and not Hayes had won Florida.

Such was the state of play when the electors met in their respective state capitals on December 6, 1876 to formally cast their ballots for the presidency. In Florida, South Carolina, and Louisiana, both the Democratic and Republican electors met and cast conflicting votes. In Oregon, both the Hayes and Tilden supporter cast a ballot. Thus, at the end of the day, four states forwarded two sets of returns to Washington to be opened by the House of Representatives.

By the time the electors met, it was clear that the Republic faced a situation never seen before. Tilden had won the popular vote by some 250,000 votes, but he did not have a clear electoral majority, having received 184 electors (one short of the 185 needed to have a majority). Meanwhile, Hayes received 165 electoral votes, leaving 20 votes in dispute. The country was facing a constitutional crisis not seen since the end of 1860, and unfortunately, the Constitution provided no clear solution. According to the Constitution, in instances where no candidate received a majority of the votes in the Electoral College, the House of Representatives would break the deadlock with each state having one vote. This had occurred in 1800 and 1824, but in 1876, there were two candidates who each claimed to have a majority of the electors. Naturally, this was not a situation that the Founders had foreseen, so in order to resolve this crisis, Congress would have to devise a solution in the absence of any precedent, and they would have to settle on one quickly because the situation threatened to get out of control and erupt in violence. Democrats were already putting forward the rallying cry, "Tilden or Blood."

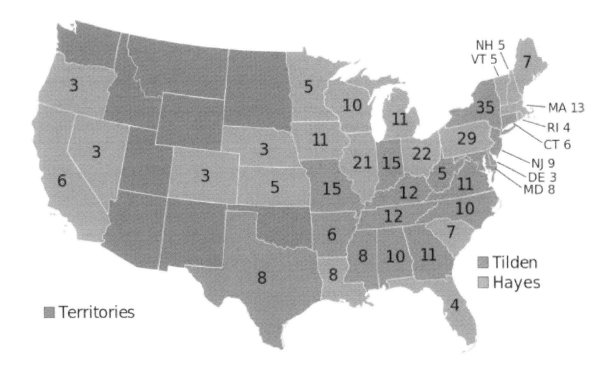

The official results of the Electoral College in 1876

   With the presidency still undecided, the capital was abuzz with reporters covering the story. Aware of Pulitzer's reputation as a political correspondent, Charles Anderson Dana, editor of the *New York Sun*, sent him to Washington to cover the dispute. Pulitzer came to admire Dana and for a time saw him as a mentor.

Dana

While in Washington, Pulitzer discovered a new distraction in his life, a pretty young woman named Kate Davis. A second cousin of Jefferson Davis, she quickly won his heart, and he spent much of 1877 winning hers. The two would be married on June 19, 1878, and naturally, their wedding announcement had flowery prose: "'Happy is the bride that the sun shines on,' is Love's proverb, and fairer sunshine June never showered upon her roses than that which all day long shone on Miss Kate Davis' wedding day. She deserved this signal favor, for a more gentle and lovely bride was never led to the altar than she who, yesterday evening, was united in marriage to the man of her choice. Miss Davis is a native of this District, a near relative of Jefferson Davis, distinguished in the society of the most cultured and refined, amid which she has moved with exceeding grace, and is regarded as its most beautiful ornament. Hon. Joseph Pulitzer, upon whom has fallen the great gift of her heart and hand, is a citizen of St. Louis, and a gentleman who has risen to distinction and wealth by the force of his own independent character both as orator and writer. They were married at the Church of the Epiphany, by the Rev. J.H.

Chew, rector of St. Alban's, Georgetown."

Kate Davis

A man of means, Pulitzer took his bride on a long honeymoon trip through Europe, but he did not leave his work behind completely. He spent much of his time tracking the social and political environments around them and composing articles to send home to be published in the *Sun*. The first of these articles appeared in the paper on September 22, 1878, and it reflected on the rise of the recently unified Germany. Prophetically, Pulitzer foresaw a coming war in Europe: "On this side of the ocean, we have passed through the worst and light is dawning. On the other, the worst is to come, and darkness with it…I cannot remember a single person of either nationality who did not clearly intimate or express a belief in the utter inevitability of another war between France and Germany. This dreadful thought was firmly impressed upon the minds of both nations. Women speak of it as a matter of course. Children are brought up in it…This may not occur for years. But it is liable to occur any day, so Bismarck thinks it necessary to be prepared for it every day. The only way to prevent war is to be amply prepared for it, seems to be the

German theory. And so that great nation enjoys a peace that is practically no peace, but only preparation for another struggle. Like gladiators or prize-fighters both Germany and France are in training for the next match. It is as ridiculous to call the present state of Germany a real peace as it would be to call the severe and trying work of training a member of the ring, pleasure. It is but a pause, not peace."

The *St. Louis Post-Dispatch* and the *New York World*

"I know that my retirement will make no difference in its cardinal principles, that it will always fight for progress and reform, never tolerate injustice or corruption, always fight demagogues of all parties, never belong to any party, always oppose privileged classes and public plunderers, never lack sympathy with the poor, always remain devoted to the public welfare, never be satisfied with merely printing news, always be drastically independent, never be afraid to attack wrong, whether by predatory plutocracy or predatory poverty." – Pulitzer's description of *The St. Louis Post-Dispatch* upon his retirement in 1907

Upon returning to America, Pulitzer began looking for a new paper to buy, and he found one in the *St. Louis Dispatch*. According to historian Denis Brian, "When the dying *St. Louis Dispatch* was up for auction on December 9, 1878, someone said 'It's not worth a damn,' another suggested forty thousand dollars. 'Not worth a damn' seemed the consensus at the auction. There were few bids, and Pulitzer topped them at twenty-five hundred dollars. He turned up at the dingy newspaper office at ten the next morning and supervised the production of the paper…The building and equipment were on their last legs. Ropes were missing to the elevator on which forms containing type were usually lowered from the composing room to the press room, so the staff improvised, carefully sliding them down the stairs. It was touch and go, but eventually some one thousand copies of the paper came off the worn and battered flatbed press. Pulitzer had budgeted twenty-seven hundred dollars to revitalize the paper. When that was exhausted, if it hadn't turned a profit, he and the *Dispatch* would be kaput…That same day, John Alvarez Dillon paid a visit. The Irish American, Harvard-educated owner of the rival Evening Post suggested combining their papers and sharing expenses and profits. Pulitzer had the advantage of a Western Associated Press franchise. He, Dillon, had the advantage of experience. Rather than destroy each other in a battle for only so many readers, why not work together? Dillon asked. Pulitzer liked the thirty-five-year-old publisher immediately and shared his progressive views and intellectual interests. He agreed to the merger on condition that in editorial policy he had the last word. Then he moved fast. Having a poor opinion of the *Dispatch* staff with one exception, Pulitzer fired the rest. He offered a job to the exception, who declined. On December 12, 1878, a reporter in the *Post's* office at 321 Pine Street looked up from his desk and saw 'a tall, distinguished looking young man (enter and look) appraisingly about, I knew without being told that it was Joseph Pulitzer. He was more than six feet tall and wore rimless glasses, a soft hat and a blue chinchilla overcoat, obviously tailored in New York.'"

From the beginning, Pulitzer insisted his new paper would be like no other paper before it. He announced, "The *Post-Dispatch* will serve no party but the people; be no organ of Republicanism, but the organ of truth; will follow no causes bit its conclusions; will not support the Administration, but criticize it; will oppose all frauds and shams wherever or whatever they are; will advocate principles and ideas rather than prejudices and partisanship."

Of course, there was more to it than that, because no matter how many platitudes Pulitzer claimed to aspire to, he fully intended to sell a lot of papers by giving the people what he knew in his heart they really wanted: dramatic, exciting, and lurid stories that no one else was publishing. As he once insisted, "If a newspaper is to be of real service to the public, it must have a big circulation: first, because its news and its comments must reach the largest possible number of people; second, because circulation means advertising, and advertising means money, and money means independence."

Biographer Iris Noble explained what this focus meant when it came to actually running the paper: "He hired a new reporter, trained him to write dramatically and taught him to go out and hunt for stories in the same way the young Joseph Pulitzer had done for the old *Westliche Post* with this difference: this reporter knew his stories would not be censored for any political, religious or financial allegiance of the publisher's. … Gambling and vice in St. Louis were Joseph's next targets. … Pulitzer found another artist and he edged close to libel suits when the drawings featured, unmistakably, the faces of well-known gambling figures. In a couple of weeks the *Post-Dispatch* had literally run the St. Louis Lottery Company out of town and won the gratitude of families who had seen husbands spend the grocery money on the faro tables or in a thousand-to-one shot on a lottery ticket…Editorially, Pulitzer followed the gambling stories with outright attacks on the city government, on real estate companies, on the lottery outfit itself anyone who was in any way involved in permitting gambling to flourish in the city. That campaign finished, he turned to a demand that the city streets be cleaned and repaired. Many were nothing but hog wallows. His articles, also, were responsible for the beginning of a park system in St. Louis…Circulation climbed every week. … Pulitzer knew it was neither accident nor miracle. It was the result of hard work. … The *Post-Dispatch* succeeded only because its editor risked both his health in long hours of hard work and risked his safety for his principles."

Business took on greater urgency since Pulitzer had a growing family to support. On June 11, 1879, less than two weeks before their first wedding anniversary, Kate gave birth to a son, Ralph, who would go on to follow in his father's footsteps in the family business. Just over a year later, a daughter named Lucille Irma joined the family. Katherine Ethyl was born in 1882, but died just two years later of pneumonia. Joseph, Jr. was born in 1885, and he would also find a career in publishing. Edith was born less than two years after that, and as an adult, she married William Scoville Moore, a real estate broker who worked with President Franklin Roosevelt to establish the Warm Springs Foundation in Georgia. She would outlive all her siblings, including Constance Helen, born in 1888, and Herbert, born in 1896.

Ralph Pulitzer

For Pulitzer, there was more to his plan than just making money. As one 2005 article observed, "As an idealist, Pulitzer thought a newspaper could uplift its readers through its editorial page. As a realist, he knew that nobody bought a paper for its editorials. To draw readers into his editorial page, he first had to lure them with his front page. ... Later generations of Post-Dispatch editors would sniff at sensationalism as beneath their dignity. But the original Pulitzer wallowed in sensationalism. Undignified, but it sold a lot of papers. He also brought something new to newspapers: the reformist crusade. And readership soared when the crusade took on a sensationalist edge -- for example, singling out by name those in the city's elite who had fudged on their personal property taxes."

Indeed, the profitable stories were something of a means to an end, with Pulitzer himself asserting, "You may write the most sublime philosophy, but if nobody reads it, where are you? You must go for your million circulation, and, when you have got it, turn the minds and the votes of your readers one way or the other at critical moments."

It is said that those who live by the sword will die by the sword, and Pulitzer's business occasionally paid dearly for its sensationalized stories. According to historian Hy B. Turner, "The paper increased its circulation steadily until an incident threatened its success. Col. John Albert Cockerill was Pulitzer's managing editor when the *Post-Dispatch* opposed the election of Col. James O. Broadhead to Congress in 1882. His law partner, Alonzo W. Slayback, entered Cockerill's office about a month before election day. An argument ensued, and the editor pulled out a revolver and fatally shot Slayback. No action was taken against Cockerill because authorities concluded that the slain man had entered the office with belligerent intent. But the city was aroused, Pulitzer's enemies blamed him, and circulation tumbled. Cockerill withdrew from the *Post-Dispatch*, and the journal slowly regained readers."

Pulitzer was so involved in his work that it seems his personal health was tied to the vitality of his newspaper. The scandal took a terrible toll on him physically, and his doctors prescribed a Mediterranean cruise, hoping that he would recover in a place far from the worries of work. He agreed to their suggestion and set sail in early 1883, but his plans changed when he stopped in New York to have a look around at the way news was reported in the big city. Turner continued, "He found that no strong paper there advocated the principles of the Democratic Party. The *Times* and *Tribune* were Republican, and the *Sun* and *Herald* went their independent ways. The *World* pretended under [Jay] Gould to hew to the Democratic philosophy, but the public knew he used his paper only to further his speculations. He did not want the journal, and the stench of his name kept down circulation. The *World* had no influence to speak of and was losing about $40,000 a year. Pulitzer could not resist the temptation of owning a paper in the country's largest city. He became excited when he heard that Gould wanted to unload the *World*. The railroad wrecker named an exorbitant price of $346,000, but Pulitzer quickly agreed. He wanted a daily that would challenge Park Row's mightiest. It mattered not to Pulitzer that the purchase price included Gould's losses, the paper's so-called 'good will,' and equipment, while the seller would only lease the building to him."

Gould

James B. Townsend, a reporter for the *World,* had been out of town during this time, and when he returned to work, he found everything had changed. Up until that time, according to author James Morris, the *World* "produced a dignified and subdued tally of the latest goings-on in American politics, foreign capitals, finance, and polite society that was consumed by those with the economic wherewithal to spend as much as a nickel…When Townsend had left, a few days earlier, the *World* was on its last legs, and appeared unlikely to be rescued by its owner, the financier Jay Gould. Townsend, one of the few reporters still with the paper, was startled by what he found upon reaching the *World's* offices." Townsend recalled, "It seemed as if a cyclone had entered the building, completely disarranged everything, and had passed away leaving confusion…"

From that day forward, most of the employees arriving for work in the morning found Pulitzer already there and hard at work, often speaking in terms that shocked even hardnosed reporters. One of those who worked for him during this period observed that Pulitzer's "speech was so interlarded with sulphurous and searing phrases that the whole staff shuddered. He was the first man I ever heard who split a word to insert an oath. He did it often. His favorite was 'indegod-dampendent.'"

The staff soon realized that they had better put aside any lackadaisical habits they had left over from the days of Gould's ownership, because Pulitzer would not tolerate them. Morris explained, "At first, Pulitzer sought solely to inculcate in his staff the principles by which he believed a paper should be written and edited. This effort, however modest it may seem, is how the *World* began on its path to becoming the most widely read newspaper in American history. (To match the reach, in comparative terms, of the million copy circulation of Pulitzer's World, today's New York Times would have to increase its paid readership by 300 percent.) In an era when the printed word ruled supreme and 1,028 daily newspapers across the country vied for readers, content was the means of competition. The medium was not the message; the message was."

In just a few short months, Pulitzer had the paper turning a comfortable profit, and in time, the *World* would become one of the most profitable papers in American history. He accomplished this by making sure everyone understood that he and he alone would be making decisions concerning all aspects of the paper. He also declared that the *World* would be "dedicated to the cause of the people rather than that of purse-potentates— devoted more to the news of the New than the Old World—that will expose all fraud and sham, fight all public evils and abuses—that will serve and battle for the people with earnest sincerity." On another occasion, he assured his readers, "Our aristocracy is the aristocracy of labor. The man who by honest, earnest toil supports his family in respectability … maintaining his good name through privations and temptations, and winning from his children respect as well as love, is the proudest aristocracy in the American republic. The new *World* is his organ."

One of the major changes Pulitzer made to the *World* was its look. Turner noted, "The nameplate was changed from Roman to Old English type. Twin hemispheres in the title, ordered out by Gould, were reinstated, and an old-fashioned printing press furnished a vignette setting. More readable type was used, and "ears," or boxes in circular style, were placed on either side of the paper's name on the front page within the first month—something unheard of in journalism."

Pulitzer's plan was simple and direct. Morris observed, "The paper abandoned its old front-page headlines. BENCH SHOW OF DOGS: PRIZES AWARDED ON THE SECOND DAY OF THE MEETING IN MADISON SQUARE GARDEN, which appeared on May 10 in the last editions before Pulitzer assumed control, was succeeded on May 12 by SCREAMING FOR MERCY: HOW THE CRAVEN CORNETTI MOUNTED THE SCAFFOLD…Two weeks later, the *World's* readers were greeted with the words BAPTIZED IN BLOOD, atop a story that, with the aid of a diagram, detailed how…people were crushed to death in a human stampede when panic broke out in a crowd enjoying a Sunday stroll on the newly opened Brooklyn Bridge. Pulitzer's dramatic headlines made the *World* stand out from its competitors like a racehorse among draft horses."

To his credit, Pulitzer rarely failed to deliver on a story as promised, and as Morris put it, he "admonished his staff to write in a buoyant, colloquial style consisting of simple nouns, bright verbs, and short, punchy sentences. The 'Pulitzer formula,' if there was one, was a story written so simply that anyone could read it, and so colorfully that no one would forget it." As Pulitzer put it, "The question, 'Did you see that in the *World*?' should be asked every day, and something should be designed to cause this."

Morris concluded, "The World's stories were animated not just by the facts the reporters dug up but also by the voices of the city they recorded. Pulitzer drove his staff to aggressively seek out interviews, a relatively new technique in journalism. Leading figures of the day, accustomed to a high wall of privacy, were affronted by what Pulitzer proudly called 'the insolence and impertinence of the reporters for the World.' Not only did he have the temerity to dispatch his men to pester politicians, manufacturers, bankers, and society figures for answers to endless questions, he also instructed them to return with specific observations. Vagueness was a sin. A tall man stood six feet two inches. A beautiful woman had auburn hair, hazel eyes, and demure lips that occasionally turned upward in a coy smile. Pulitzer had an uncanny ability to recognize news in what others ignored. He sent out reporters to mine the urban dramas his competitors consigned to their back pages. … Pulitzer pushed his writers to think like Charles Dickens, who wove fiction from sad tales of Victorian London, to create compelling entertainment from the drama of the modern city. … The World drew in…readers, many of whom were immigrants struggling to master their first words of English. Writing about the events that mattered in their lives in a way they could understand, Pulitzer's World gave these New Yorkers a feeling of belonging and a sense of value. The moneyed class learned to pick up the World with trepidation. Each day brought a fresh assault on privilege. In one stroke, Pulitzer simultaneously elevated the common man and took his spare change."

While the news may have been sensationalized, Pulitzer maintained dignity and clarity in his editorials, believing that it was up to him to inspire his readers to better themselves and the nation. In 1883, he declared, "We will always fight for progress and reform, never tolerate injustice or corruption, always fight demagogues of all parties, always oppose privileged classes and public plunderers, never lack sympathy with the poor, always remain devoted to the public welfare, never be satisfied with merely printing news, always be drastically independent, never be afraid to attack wrong, whether by predatory plutocracy or predatory poverty."

These were the halcyon days of newspaper men, as New York City was growing at the fastest rate in its history, and many new improvements, such as the Brooklyn Bridge, enabled Pulitzer to expand his circulation and improve delivery. He did, however, rail against the penny toll pedestrians were charged to cross, complaining, "The people demand a free bridge. They have had to pay for its construction, it is said, several times over…The working classes of the city do not enjoy many privileges. Let them at least have free schools, free air, free daylight and a free bridge."

This was the first of many cries Pulitzer issued on behalf of the common man. Writing to Frank Cobb, Pulitzer told him, "Generally speaking, always remember the difference between a paper made for the millions, for the masses, and a paper made for the classes. In using the word masses, I do not exclude anybody. I should make a paper that the judges of the Supreme Court of the United States would read with enjoyment, everybody, but I would not make a paper that only the judges of the Supreme Court and their class would read. I would make this paper without lowering the tone in the slightest degree."

Not surprisingly, Pulitzer's efforts earned him plenty of criticism from his rivals, but the attack from his former friend Dana must have stung a little more than the rest. Dana said that while Pulitzer "possesses a quick and fluent mind, with a good share of originality and brightness…he has always seemed to us rather deficient in judgment and in staying power." Furious, Pulitzer lashed back at Dana, writing, "It may have been bad judgment on the part of Mr. Dana to employ the present editor of The World as a correspondent for his paper, but if the editor of The World has shown deficiency of judgment in journalism heretofore, it has been because he had tried not only to imitate but even to excel the Sun in its truthfulness, fearlessness, independence, and vigor."

Inevitably, Pulitzer's attitudes about the news and his paper trickled down to his staff. Turner noted, "They intruded on rightfully shielded property, drummed upon the emotions of the unfortunate, and exploited the vices of humanity more brazenly than readers had known in decades." As a result, the *World* carried "stories [that] appealed to the masses: stories of sex, money, murder, and success; stories of the powerful and the rich who dealt in corruption; and stories of the weak who were not always in the right and whom he could frown upon but champion."

To make room for such stories, Pulitzer expanded his paper to 10 pages, and 12 on Sundays. Philip Pearl, one of Pulitzer's best reporters, remembered what it was like at the peak of the paper's popularity: "The *World* was read in Harlem, in Hell's Kitchen, in the colleges, on the East Side, in Greenwich Village, and, especially, in all newspaper off ices. It appealed alike to the intelligent and the simple because it was imbued with a fundamental sympathy. It had a heart. It had courage. It was interested in events chiefly as they affected human beings. At times it grew maudlin over life's little tragedies or great joys. But it could never treat them matter-of-factly…The World did not attempt to print all the news. For this it was branded as something less than a newspaper. Of course, it always gloried in being a good deal more than a newspaper. But, save in breathless spurts, it couldn't approach the completeness, the mechanical precision and the impersonal proficiency of the Times. It lacked method and organization and direction.… [but] Out of the daily chaos there evolved a live, readable newspaper, usually well-written and well-balanced."

While he juggled all these new responsibilities, Pulitzer never lost his interest in politics, and he once boasted, "I can never be elected president because I am a foreigner, but someday I am going to elect a president." In a sense, he made good on this promise in November 1884, when his hard work on behalf of Grover Cleveland made Cleveland the first Democrat elected to the White House since James Buchanan in 1856. Cleveland credited Pulitzer for his victory, writing some years later, "The contest was so close it may be said without reservation that if it had lacked the forceful and potent advocacy of Democratic principles at that time by the *New York World* the result might have been reversed."

1884 also saw Pulitzer elected to Congress from New York's Ninth District. However, as was often the case for 19th century writers, he soon learned that politics was more interesting and fun from the outside looking in than from the inside looking out. He resigned on his 39th birthday after just four months in office, claiming that his governing duties were taking too much time away from his work as a publisher.

One of the reasons that Pulitzer found himself so busy lay in the fact that the *World's* circulation nearly doubled following the election, topping 220,000 papers a day. At the same time, Dana's paper also peaked briefly, but then went into a decline.

Pulitzer remained grateful for the life and success he enjoyed in America, and in 1885, he had a chance to show his appreciation. The Statue of Liberty had been conceived of as a project many years before by Frédéric Auguste Bartholdi, who was struck by the size and location of Bedloe's Island, which arriving and departing ships sailed past. He described his thoughts at the time: "In the course of the voyage I formed some conceptions of a plan of a monument, but I can say that at the view of the harbor of New York the definite plan was first clear to my eyes. The picture that is presented to the view when one arrives at New York is marvelous; when, after some days of voyaging, in the pearly radiance of a beautiful morning is revealed the magnificent spectacle of those immense cities, of those rivers extending as far as the eye can reach, festooned with masts and flags; when one awakes, so to speak, in the midst of that interior sea covered with vessels, some giants in size, some dwarfs, which swarm about, puffing, whistling, swinging the great arms of their uncovered walking-beams, moving to and fro like a crowd upon a public place. It is thrilling. It is, indeed, the New World, which appears in its majestic expanse, with the ardor of its glowing life."

Bartholdi

According to *Harper's Weekly*, "The ground was first broken for the erection of the pedestal in April, 1883; the excavation was begun in June; the laying of the foundation in October; and work was continued until December, 1884 — a period of eighteen months. Work was again begun on May 11, 1885, and the work will not be completed before it will have required nearly two years of continuous labor of as many men as can work on it The stone is from a quarry on Leete's Island in Connecticut, and the white-ness of the rough quoins gives a pleasant effect at a distance of several miles. These quoins are so heavy that the labor of lifting them to such a height has made the building of the pedestal one of the heaviest pieces of masonry ever done, even. In the vicinity of New York, where the piers of the East River Bridge stand as monuments of massive stone work. The total cost will not be less than $250,000. Colonel Charles P. Stone, the engineer-in-chief, has as large a force of men as can work on the structure at once, and it will be finished as rapidly as possible. The pedestal has been built to stand for all time to come."

However, even as the newly completed Statue of Liberty was destined to arrive in America and be assembled, the work on the pedestal was at an impasse over funding. In an editorial published on March 16, 1885, the *New York World* told readers, "The Statue was to be a gift emblematic of our attainment of the first century of independence. The Congress has refused to appropriate the necessary money and has thrown the responsibilities back to the American people. It (the statue) is not a gift from the millionaires of France to the millionaires of America but a gift of the whole people of France to the whole people of America. It is meant for every reader of the world. Give something, however little…There is but one thing that can be done. We must raise the money! The World is the people's paper, and it now appeals to the people to come forward and raise this money. The $250,000 that the making of the Statue cost was paid in by the masses of the French people—by the workingmen, the tradesmen, the shop girls, the artisans—by all, irrespective of class or condition. Let us respond in like manner. Let us not wait for the millionaires to give this money. It is not the gift from the millionaires of France to the millionaires of America, but a gift of the whole people of France to the whole people of America."

Still worried about the possibility that another city might yet take the statue from New York City, Pulitzer offered to publish the name of anyone who gave any donation, great or small. Over the next several months, various notes appeared in its pages referencing those who donated to the cause. For example, the paper cited a " young girl alone in the world" who donated "60 cents, the result of self-denial," the donation of "five cents as a poor office boy's mite toward the Pedestal Fund," as well as a dollar sent by children from "the money we saved to go to the circus with." Even a group of men living in a home for alcoholics raised $15.

Turner explained the effect Pulitzer's pleas had: "That was the opening plea. Money started coming in, with amounts as low as five cents. The paper offered prizes to those sending in the largest contributions. First prize would be two double gold eagles, or $40 in gold, and a total of $100 would be distributed. … Pulitzer published the names of all contributors, some of their letters, and notices of affairs given for the fund's benefit…Children, servant girls, longshoremen, newsboys, clerks, cab drivers, and laborers took part in the crusade. Within four months, the fund was completed. More than 120,000 persons contributed the needed $100,000."

On August 11, 1885, the *New York World* joyfully exclaimed that more than $100,000 had been raised, with the vast majority of the donations coming from people giving a dollar or less. As the money continued to come in, work on the pedestal began again. While it was originally hoped the pedestal could be made of solid granite, those funding the project suggested rather forcefully that the laborers look for a less expensive option, so Lady Liberty has always stood on concrete walls that are faced with granite. That said, this base was impressive in its own right, as its 20 feet thick walls were the largest poured up until that time in history.

On June 17, 1885, the steamer Isère arrived in New York Harbor from France bearing her precious cargo. More than 200,000 people stood along the docks or went out in boats to watch the ship arrive, but even at this point, the pedestal was not yet ready (and would not be until the spring of 1886). Nevertheless, the pieces of the statue began to be uncrated and taken to the island to be reassembled. Steel I-beams were first anchored into the concrete to hold the Lady's iron bones in place, and when this was completed, her beautiful copper skin was carefully attached. The size and shape of the statue made it impossible to use scaffolding, so the workers attached the copper into place while hanging from ropes.

A painting depicting the arrival of the statue in New York Harbor

The Statue of Liberty may have been one of his pet projects, but it took up only a small part of Pulitzer's time. In fact, most of his time was spent dealing with more controversial issues. For instance, during this period, he was involved in an effort to uncover what became known as the Broadway Boodle Ring. Apparently, the wealthy owner of the Seventh Avenue Railway, Jacob Sharp, was determined to place streetcars up and down Broadway. However, many businessmen in the area opposed the idea, perhaps because the cars would carry potential shoppers past their stores, when they otherwise would have to walk up sidewalks and potentially stop in to shop. In order to obtain his goals, Sharp spent hundreds of thousands of dollars bribing aldermen to vote to give him the franchise.

At first, the stories of bribes and shady dealings seemed impossible to prove, but Pulitzer assigned some of his best reporters to ferret out evidence, and they soon came back with enough information to help bring about a grand jury investigation. The jury indicted Sharp and most of the Board of Aldermen of New York, information that Pulitzer gleefully shared with his readers.

Those aldermen who could left town to avoid trial, while many who stayed were arrested and convicted of their crimes, as was Sharp himself. It was one of Pulitzer's greatest triumphs.

Pulitzer also broke new ground in journalism by hiring a new "girl reporter," a 22 year old woman writing under the pen name Nellie Bly. Originally from the *Pittsburgh Dispatch*, Bly had come to New York in 1887 seeking excitement and the opportunity to write about something more than society and fashion. She had already made something of a name for herself by spending six months in Mexico and angering the Mexican government by uncovering the way it treated prisoners in its jails.

Bly

Bly persuaded Pulitzer not only to hire her, but to give her an exciting assignment. Eventually, it was decided that she would pretend to be mentally ill and get herself confined to the Women's Lunatic Asylum on Blackwell's Island. Professor of Journalism Diane Lamb explained how the ploy came about, writing, "The inheritor of the hijinks and homeyness of the Penny Press, Joseph Pulitzer evolved a formula that woke up the 'sleepers' in his audience with newspapers that were at once gaudy and serious. The variety in *The New York World* showed how multifaceted sensationalism can be at its best. Pulitzer had big headlines, color and cartoons, an intellectual editorial page, great investigative articles, and enough stunts to choke a circus. He said, yes, when Nellie Bly proposed going into Blackwell's Insane Asylum as a patient in order to expose conditions there. No one had ever gone undercover in a mental hospital before, much less a woman. Mental hospitals weren't even considered fit subjects for journalism, although Pulitzer's readers formed the poverty population from which its patients were drawn. … Most of the people in his audience were immigrants or the children of immigrants. They were poorly educated and used to receiving information by the spoken word. They were not fundamentally print-oriented. They did not see their lives reflected in many of the existing publications in New York before Pulitzer's arrival. They were not interested in the prestige topic of the day, i.e. politics…Most of the investigative stories that Pulitzer ran in *The World* were about problems that his readers faced themselves. Immigrant women could empathize with Louise Schanz who was committed to Blackwell's Island without a hearing, because she spoke only German. The essence of this kind of journalism is that it is performed…Bly did not interview immigrant women who were being conned into prostitution, instead she sat on a bench in Central Park and waited for the pimp to come along in his coach and four to try to pick her up. The reporter makes the story happen and is the reader's stand-in."

Bly's efforts and subsequent exposé were so popular that another ambitious effort was assigned to her, and while she took a much celebrated trip around the world over the course of 9 weeks, similar projects were given to other writers. The 20th Century editor Jim Squires explained, "The stunt was such a success she was sent around the world in search of more skullduggery and in her absence editors established a Sunday column with the fictitious byline of 'Meg Merrilies' to produce similarly lurid and grisly female reporter antics - infamous for their tearful, heart-rending prose of 'human interest with human appeal.' Male staffers often wrote the column while wearing an article of female clothing monogrammed 'MM.'"

While the *New York World* continued to have its circulation grow astronomically, other competitors tried to keep up. Charles Dana expanded to publish a second paper each day, launching the *Evening Sun* in 1887. Not to be outdone, Pulitzer added the *Evening World* to his stable just months later, on October 10, 1887.

Dana was so furious over this development that he joined forces with the infamous Tammany Hall to back Colonel John R. Fellows to run against Republican De Lancey Nicoll for the office of District Attorney for New York County. Dana had initially backed Nicoll, but he changed his allegiance after hearing that Pulitzer was supporting Nicoll, primarily in recognition of his good work prosecuting Sharp and his cronies.

Nicoll

In some of the most offensive pieces ever published in American newspapers, Dana attempted to tear Nicoll down by attacking Pulitzer, making sure to emphasize Pulitzer's Jewish background. On October 28, 1887, Dana's paper included this screed: "The boss behind Nicoll is Judas Pulitzer, who exudes the venom of a snake and wields a bludgeon of a bully. He has accepted the candidacy of Nicoll from the Republicans with as much thankfulness as in the days when he cringed for a nickel on the barroom floor. This Dick Turpin of journalism, this contemporary Judas has not even the sensibility of his prototype." On another occasion, the paper wrote, "'Vy? Vy? Vy?' Judas Pulitzer will shout on the day after election…. Will he be able to read the answer to his 'Vy?' in the returns? Who knows? Who cares? He will have had enough of trying to boss New York…'I vonder vere I can get some hemb cheab.—Choe Buliter.'" Dana even went as far as to declare, "Judas Pulitzer is a Jew who denies his race and pretends that he is not of Jewish origin. He is ashamed of his birth and ancestry, and tries to repudiate them. He thus makes himself a Judas indeed."

Pulitzer gave as good as he got, calling Dana "the champion liar of America" and accusing him of having an "infamous blackguard." But in the end, Fellows won the race, leading Dana to crow, "We wish, Pulitzer, that you had never come. Perhaps your lot will be like that of the mythical unfortunate of the race you belong to and deny … we mean the Wandering Jew. In that case, it may shortly please the inscrutable Providence which has chastened us with your presence, to give you that stern and dreadful signal—Move on, Pulitzer, move on!"

Pulitzer responded by hitting Dana where it hurt: "The editor of the World accepts the hatred of Mr. Dana as a compliment…He especially appreciates the agonized heart-cry of Mr. Dana, which appears in yesterday's issue of the Sun, in the midst of a literary muck-heap, which could only be found on the editorial page of that paper: 'We wish, Pulitzer, that you had never come.' Nothing could be truer than this. From his innermost soul the broken and humiliated editor of the Sun wishes that the regeneration of the World had never taken place. In four years' time he has seen the circulation of his paper dwindle until it has fallen into the third rank; he has seen his dividends vanish; his income swept away…Sad, no doubt, Mr. Dana is, that somebody came who could provide the New York public with the newspaper which it wanted. But the man is here, and he will remain. The World is stronger and better today than it ever was."

In spite of Pulitzer's defiant words, the stress of the campaign and his feud had taken its toll and led him to the brink of a nervous breakdown. His eyesight was also worse, strained as it was from too many late nights studying proofs. And then, there were his concerns over the Evening Edition. At first, the evening paper cost three cents and featured a higher, more conservative tone than its morning counterpart. However, it not only lost money itself, but also hurt the morning edition's circulation. Pulitzer struggled for two years to make it profitable before giving up and ordering his employees to return to the price and style of the morning edition. From that time onward, the paper sold well, soon surpassing the *Evening Sun*.

As Pulitzer aged, he still remained a force to be reckoned with in the office, leading one of his staff to remark, "He was the damnedest best man in the world to have in a newspaper office for one hour in the morning. For the remainder of the day he was a damned nuisance." However, his mood took a marked turn for the worse in 1887 when his already poor eyesight suddenly began to decline further. He also developed a number of emotional issues, likely related to his dismay over this loss. The most obvious of these was that he was able to tolerate only minimum noise. With newsrooms being notoriously loud and boisterous, he began to spend less time in the office and more time traveling.

Nonetheless, despite being away more often, Pulitzer became more strident in his demands concerning the stories the *World* published. Writing in *Central Ideas in the Development of American Journalism: A Narrative History*, Marvin Olasky observed, "In the early 1890s, Pulitzer stopped short of calling for outright socialism; yet, the World's constant juxtaposition of current horror with future social salvation transmitted the message of hope through science and material progress, evenly distributed by benign government agents. Features such as 'Experimenting with an Electric Needle and an Ape's Brain' showed that scientific transformation of man's thought patterns was just around the corner, and stories such as 'Science Can Wash Your Heart' suggested that immortality was possible. In the meantime, however, monstrous crime and terrible scandal rode mankind. In one sense Pulitzer was merely imitating the methodology of the Puritan press two centuries before: emphasize bad news so that the need for the good news becomes even greater. But the message was totally changed…the World portrayed itself as the battler against systemic oppression, and proposed running over anyone (including business owners in American, Spaniards in Cuba, and Boers in South Africa) who stood in the way of 'progress.'"

By this point, there seemed to be little left for Pulitzer to do but leave the newspaper business altogether, or at least to leave the place where the paper was created. Thus, in 1890, though he was only 43 years old, he gave up his position as editor of *The World* and began to use his wealth to travel throughout the world, again and again consulting doctors and specialists about some drug or treatment that could restore his health and allow him to live a normal life again. Near the end of his life, Pulitzer would note, Whatever my trouble had been at first, it developed into separation of the retina in both eyes. From the day on which I first consulted the oculist up to the present time, about twenty-four years, I have only been three times in 'The World' building. Most people think I'm dead or living in Europe in complete retirement."

However, even after giving up the position, as David Davidson later wrote in an article for *American Heritage* magazine, "Pulitzer had no intention of abandoning his newspaper to other hands…he made elaborate arrangements with a corps of six secretary-companions who picked up preshipped batches of the World at every stop along the route of his travels, read every line of every news story to him, and took dictation of an endless flow of telegrams, cables, and letters that praised or scolded the handling of every major article and editorial." Obviously, this was not easy work, and it's fair to wonder how many people even wanted the job, but Pulitzer was unwilling to settle for anything less than excellence. Davidson continued, "These secretary-companions had to go through a rigorous process before he accepted them. Not only did he demand that they have pleasant voices, a cheerful manner, and refrain from the forbidden noises, they also were put through a stiff interrogation on the arts, the sciences, political affairs, literature, and world problems. By this system he continued to edit the World closely from his numerous homes…abroad in Paris and London; from his yacht Liberty."

Some people have considered Pulitzer's behavior at this time to have been paranoid, but to be fair, he was dealing with issues concerning one of the most powerful newspapers in the United States. As Davidson noted, "To keep private all telegraphed and cabled messages, Pulitzer created twenty thousand code names and words. He dubbed himself Andes….Woodrow Wilson was Melon, …and President Cleveland was Graving. A typical coded message read: Continue Mohican assistant Gruesome making Gushless Gruesome during Glorify's vacation. This translated as: Continue Charles Lincoln as assistant managing editor, making Oliver K. Bovard managing editor during J. J. Spurgeon's vacation."

Hearst's Early Years

William Randolph Hearst was born on April 29, 1863, to newlyweds George and Phoebe Apperson Hearst. His father, as he was always proud to say, was a pioneer who came to California during the Gold Rush and made and lost a number of fortunes throughout his lifetime. His mother was even more unique, an independent woman who at 19 agreed to marry the 41-year-old George, but only after receiving certain considerations. On June 14, 1862, the day before they were married by a local minister, the two signed and registered the following prenuptial agreement at the Crawford County Courthouse in Steelville, Missouri: "This marriage contract made & entered into this 14th day of June, 1862 between, George Hearst of the one part & Phebe E. Eperson [sic] of the other part both of the County of Franklin & State of Missouri "to wit." The parties to this instrument in consideration of the covenants & stipulation hereinafter mentiones promises & agrees to intermarry with each other within a reasonable and convenient time after the execution hereof. 2. The said George Hearst in consideration of said future marriage hereby for himself conveys assigns & sits over unto the said Phebe E. Eperson Fifty Shares of stock in the Goaldine & Curry Gold and Silver Mining Company of Virginia City Nevada Territory U.S. out of this interest which said Hearst had in said Mining Company to be held for & during the natural life of said Phebe E. Eperson and at her death revert to the said George Hearst his heirs or legal representatives."

George Hearst

Phoebe Hearst

When William was born, Phoebe assumed that he would be the first of many children. With that in mind, as well as the cultural norms of the mid-19ᵗʰ century, she left Willie, as they called him, with a nurse while she continued on with her own pursuits. According to Hearst biographer David Nasaw, "For the next twenty years, George and Phoebe Hearst would be apart far more than they would be together. Both, if we can believe their letters, suffered from the arrangement, but Phoebe had the more difficult time, at least at first. George was at home in the West and had become accustomed to the predominantly male world of the mining camps. Phoebe was new to the West, new to city life, and a young mother."

At the same time, it seems that George truly loved his young wife and cared about at least her physical comfort. In early 1864, Phoebe and Willie moved into an elegant new home on Chestnut Street in San Francisco purchased for them by George, but they made the move on their own as George remained at mining camps hundreds of miles away. In addition, she was about to lose her parents, who themselves were moving to a farm near Santa Clara (also purchased by

George).

In order to focus on the move, Phoebe sent Willie with his nurse, Eliza Pike, to Santa Cruz in early June. During this separation, Phoebe wrote many letters to Eliza, many filled with angst and drama that reflect the flightiness of a young mother barely out of her teens: "It seems a month since you left. I am terribly lonely, I miss Baby every minute. I think and dream about him. We all feel lost…I have had another letter from Mr. Hearst…he expects to be home soon, but don't say what he means by soon, a week, or a month…Kiss Willie for me and write me how he is. I hope you will wean him…I am going to telegraph Mr. Hearst to know what to do about moving up on the hill, we have only two weeks more. I don't think I can come down to see you I will be so very busy. Write often. I feel anxious to hear from you. Oh dear what am I going to do."

In time, Phoebe grew into her new role, and Nasaw noted that, with George gone so much, "Phoebe adjusted to life as a single mother. She learned to make decisions by herself, run the household, and raise Willie. She was assisted of course by her husband's wealth, which provided her with a household filled with servants and the incentive and leisure to educate herself - and her boy."

As time passed and no other children came along to join her growing son, she became quite a doting mother, and one who some might characterize as obsessive. In 1871, Phoebe wrote to a friend, "I take great pleasure in amusing and interesting him at home so that he may be kept as much as possible from bad children. Of course, I must allow him to have company often but I manage to watch them closely. So far he is a very innocent child and I mean to keep him so just as long as I can…He is a great comfort to us. Mr. Hearst is so proud of him and too indulgent to try to keep from spoiling him…Mr. Hearst often says he would not like to have Willie on a jury if his Mama was concerned, for whether it was justice or not, he would decide in my favor…I am so sorry we have no other children. We love babies so dearly, why we are not blessed I cannot understand…I have had the dressing room adjoining my bedroom all fixed up for Willie, a nice bed put up. It is a pretty little room and so near me, he is very much pleased."

Two years later, when he was still just 10 years old and had only been in school for two years, Phoebe removed young Willie from school again to take him on an extended trip to Europe. While the trip itself would obviously be extremely educational for an impressionable young child, Phoebe also arranged for him to have regular lessons in all his academic subjects. With that said, her motivation for taking him does not seem to necessarily have been his best interests as much as her own need. From her letters, it becomes clear that, while George and Phoebe Hearst had a very good marriage, she needed nearly constant companionship and often turned to her son for company when her husband was working the long hours needed to support them and improve the family's circumstances.

As it turned out, the family's fortunes took a downturn during the Panic of 1873, while Phoebe and Willie were in Europe, and when they returned home in October 1874, George, at Phoebe's suggestion, had sold their home on Chestnut Street. The family would spend the coming years in one rented space after another, even though their circumstances were always quite comfortable.

By this time, George Hearst was known on the West Coast as both an outstanding prospector and excellent judge of mining properties. He certainly enjoyed gambling both in business and for pleasure, though not in excess. In the mid-1870s, he accepted a small newspaper called the *San Francisco Examiner* as a payment of a gambling debt a friend owed him, and he would pass this company on to Willie about a decade later, setting in motion his son's rise to publishing royalty. All the while, the sense of instability brought on by moving from place to place and school to school may have led the younger Hearst to develop a passion for acquiring material possessions that would mark the rest of his life.

As the son of a wealthy and prominent man now involved in state and national politics, it was important to his family that the only Hearst heir receive an excellent education, one that was not available to him in California. Thus, his parents shipped him off across country to be educated in New England. After finishing a tenure at St. Paul's School in Concord, New Hampshire, Hearst enrolled in Harvard College in 1880. According to a 1951 article published in *The Harvard Crimson*, "During his three College years, Hearst had an opportunity to display some of the publishing talent that later built the greatest newspaper empire ever known in America. His field of activity was modest--the Harvard Lampoon. He took over as business manager of the funny magazine when it was laboring under heavy arrears of debt, and in two years transformed it into a paying proposition." George Santayana, who also served as an editor of the *Lampoon*, remembered, "The fact that his father was a millionaire and a Senator from California gave him an independence that disturbed the undergraduate mind, and his long cigars were bad form in the Yard. Yet his budding prowess as a newspaper owner and manager made him invaluable to the Lampoon in its financial straits."

The article also made reference to one of Hearst's less noble acts, one that may have led to his early departure from college. Hearst expressed his interest in collecting art too early and too casually, and his gifts to several professors of their visages etched on the bottom of chamber-pots proved that Harvard did not have the West's sense of humor. Young Hearst was invited to leave Harvard a year before graduating, and returned to California in disgrace.

Once back home, Willie's mother made sure that he suffered no serious repercussions for his lapses, even while his father insisted that he had to find something useful to do with his life. After drifting along for a couple of years, in 1887 Hearst persuaded his father (who by that time had become a U.S. Senator from California) to make him the editor of the *Examiner*. Writing a few decades later, journalist Robert Duffuss observed, "Everyone knew that a youngster like this was certain to make a failure of newspaper work, and it was his father's newspaper which he had chosen for his plaything. There was even reason to suspect that the Senator himself entertained few delusions on the subject. The only question was how long the money would last and what toy the amateur editor would take up next when the varnish had worn off this one."

Hearst soon proved them wrong, and with near unlimited funding from his parents, he made sure the "Monarch of the Dailies" had the best of everything, from equipment to writers. He also began to publish stories that sought to uncover both private and political corruption.

Among those he brought on board to investigate the shady dealings was a somewhat notorious author who had already demonstrated his journalistic skills in other California papers. Writing on September 4, 1889, Ambrose Bierce held readers in the palm of his hand as he observed some inconsistencies present in a local murder trial: "Redwood City, the town from which Mr. Powell thought it expedient to remove Editor Ralph Smith, has the distinction and advantage of numbering among its "prominent citizens" two brothers named Ross, one of whom is an ornament to the legal profession; the other adorns the medical. At the time when Mr. Powell sated his desire for the absence of Editor Smith by shooting him down in cold blood when he was unarmed, the medical Ross held the office of coroner and naturally conducted an inquest with a view to ascertaining if anyone was in fault. The post mortem examination showing that only two of Mr. Powell's bullets had penetrated the body, and that only one of these had done any damage…seems to have convinced Dr. Ross, the coroner, that Mr. Powell's connection with the matter was too slight really to implicate him in a murder; for he straightway went upon his bail bond…Possibly Dr. Ross may have been able more clearly to discern his duty to go upon Mr. Powell's bail bond by the broad beam of revelation thrown upon that gentleman's innocence by Lawyer Ross' retention for the defense. The Ross blood is apparently a good deal thicker than water—thicker even than the blood of poor Ralph Smith, upon the hands of Mr. Powell." Bierce concluded, "We cannot, of course, say with certainly whether Ross was influenced by fraternal considerations in standing by his brother's client; his belief in Mr. Powell's blameless intentions in shooting down an unarmed and comparatively weak man and shooting him after he was down…may sufficiently account for his act. To accuse such a man of fraternal feeling, or feeling of any kind, is going pretty far." Needless to say, this type of hype sold papers, and the *Examiner* was soon among the most popular papers in San Francisco.

With the money he was now making, Hearst decided to build himself a home of his own near Pleasanton, California, though it must be noted he built the home on land owned by his father and his mother ended up taking over the project. Nonetheless, it was still his home, and he named it Hacienda del Pozo de Verona. Writing for *Diablo* magazine in 2006, Susan Davis vividly described the estate: "[Phoebe's] husband bought the 500-acre property in 1886 but died shortly thereafter, in 1891. William Randolph then started to convert the ranch house on the property into a hunting lodge. Hearst feared that her son was going to use it to entertain his rough friends, so she took over the project. She also wanted more than a hunting lodge. A long-time supporter of women's advancement, she hired Julia Morgan, the first female architecture student at the prestigious Ecole des Beaux-Arts in Paris and the first licensed female architect in

California. It would take more than a decade to complete Hearst's mansion, but it ended up being one of the most magnificent homes in America. Hacienda del Pozo de Verona was named after a 15th-century carved-stone wellhead (pozzo means well in Italian) that William Randolph had shipped from Verona, Italy. The house was a showcase from the moment a visitor stepped into its large entry courtyard and was greeted by the sight of the ornate wellhead serving as a large fountain. Inside, Hearst exhibited her massive collection of artwork and furniture, as well as artifacts from around the world that she picked up on her travels…The main building was three stories and had more than 50 rooms. One of the fireplaces was large enough to spit-roast a whole ox. The estate's playhouse, designed for Hearst's five grandchildren, rose two stories high and contained 13 rooms, billiard tables, and several reading rooms. The list of guests over the years included royalty, artists, composers, presidents, and movie stars from far and wide."

Building a Publishing Empire

Hearst did not live in his new home for long. As an ambitious young man, California was only the beginning. The way he saw it, San Francisco, and even all of California itself, was too small a territory for him, so he soon turned his attention east and began to dream of owning multiple newspapers stretching across the country. With Phoebe's emotional and financial backing, Hearst purchased the *New York Morning Journal* in 1895. As he had with the *Examiner*, Hearst poured money into these establishments, hiring such prominent authors as Julian Hawthorne and Stephen Crane to write the kind of sensationalized stories made popular by the current king of journalism, Joseph Pulitzer. Not surprisingly, Pulitzer took umbrage at Hearst, especially when the newcomer stole his best illustrator, Richard Outcault. As the two entered into an all-out war for readership, Hearst slowly lured away many others from Pulitzer's staff, causing the older man no end of stress and misery.

Crane

Among the many ways in which Hearst managed to outdo Pulitzer was in how he treated his employees. Writing in *The Uncrowned King: The Sensational Rise of William Randolph Hearst*, Kenneth Whyte pointed out, "Hearst quickly established himself as the most attractive employer on the street, and a clear favorite over the suspicious and volatile Pulitzer, his chief rival for newspapering talent. Journalists responded with dedication and enterprise. They followed their proprietor's lead in subordinating all other concerns—office politics, administrative niceties, sobriety—to the overarching goal of creating a great and popular newspaper. And the Journal, effectively a new publication without a preexisting style or personality, quickly found its voice."

As he built up his reputation for being a fair and reasonable boss, Hearst was able to lure away several of Pulitzer's best editors, including Morrill Goddard, who was responsible for building interest in the growing American pastime of reading the Sunday paper. He also brought over a young man named Arthur Brisbane, who was already on his way to becoming one of the most important newspaper columnists in American history. Hearst made Brisbane the managing editor of the business.

Hearst, Robert G. Vignola, and Brisbane in 1920

In 1896, a popular trade paper, *Printer's Ink*, quoted a local advertising executive as saying, "I cannot help feeling that that man Hearst had struck it. He has done what he alone could have done. The success is as conspicuous, as mysterious, as actually present as the electric light. It is here, we see it, we know it, and it is Hearst that has done it. He has created a great property and it will grow and grow. He alone had done it. It was not his money…It was not the men he has gathered around him…but the success is attributable solely to him…." The executive in question continued, "Nothing succeeds like success, and it is upon…a phenomenal success that the young man from the other side of the continent is already rearing a colossal structure—upon a foundation already plainly seen to be wide and broad and strong enough to sustain any weight and height its projector may aspire to construct. He will do what…has not been done." Perhaps the secret of Hearst's success could be found in his paper's motto: "While Others Talk, the

Journal Acts."

Due to issues related to copyright, both the *World* and the *Journal* ran a comic series drawn by Outcault and called the *Yellow Kid*. According to one expert, the series "presented a turn-of-the-century theater of the city, in which class and racial tensions of the new urban, consumerist environment were acted out by a mischievous group of New York City kids from the wrong side of the tracks…Americans embraced the Yellow Kid during a time when commerce became central to the American way; the comic grew popular on the pages of two of the leading newspapers, and even influenced another 'clean' newspaper editor to name the papers' explicit reporting of New York City urban life 'yellow-kid journalism.'" The term stuck, and it was shortened over time to "yellow journalism," especially around the time of the Spanish-American War.

It wouldn't be possible to definitively determine who was most responsible for the radical changes that newspapers made near the end of the 19th century and the beginning of the 20th century as they transformed themselves into something like modern tabloids instead of traditional, dry sources of news. Pulitzer certainly started the trend, and he had been publishing such stories since Hearst was still in school, but Hearst, in his quest to beat Pulitzer at his own game, upped the ante, cashing in by exaggerating run-of-the-mill stories to sell papers. Ironically, as Kenneth Whyte noted, some of the sensationalism actually served the public well in some instances: "It is true that news of society and calamities were a part of the paper's formula for success. They were a part of every major Park Row daily's formula for success. … Hearst, in fact, improved the quality of crime and disaster coverage at the *Journal*. He engaged readers less with frights than by illuminating character and creating narrative by playing up the arts of police detection and courtroom argument, by delineating justice issues and moral controversies and vigoruously taking sides in them. He made similar improvements to the paper's gossip and society news, eliminating a clutch of cheesy columns with names like 'Gossip of the Swells' and the 'Jolly Joker,' in favor of Alan Dale's popular reviews and 'Caught in the Metropolitan Whirl,' a smart new column containing short, breezy observations about city life. The whole paper was being reworked. The quality of its prose, while still uneven, was improving steadily. The design, on the whole, was more polished. Coverage was more comprehensive throughout: foreign and financial news were expanded, along with sports and arts."

A picture of the *New York Journal's* coverage of the murder of Stanford White in 1906

Unable to beat Hearst at telling gripping stories, Pulitzer decided to cut his prices, reducing the cost of his papers from two cents to a penny, the price Heart charged, and before long, both men were willing to do nearly anything to outsell the other.

While newspapers today are accused of being partisan, those in the 1890s were unabashedly so, and the *Journal* was no different. Hearst made it clear that any publication with his name on it would be a populist paper, thereby supporting the more liberal principles of the Democratic Party. In fact, the *Journal* was the only major newspaper on the East Coast to back William Jennings Bryan's run for the presidency. Hearst made it his business, and that of his reporters, to ferret out any and all examples of graft or corruption in the campaign run by Republican candidate William McKinley. The most important story his team uncovered concerned Mark Hanna, who had carved out for himself a place as the first political "boss" to gain power across the nation, whereas others, such as the infamous "Boss Tweed," had merely attained local influence. According to Hanna biographer David Croly, "For a while [Hearst reporter Alfred] Lewis appears to have been stationed in Cleveland in order to tell lies about him. He was depicted as a monster of sordid and ruthless selfishness, who fattened himself and other men on the flesh and blood of the common people. This picture of the man was stamped sharply on the popular consciousness by the powerful but brutal caricatures of Homer Davenport. Day after day he was portrayed with perverted ability and ingenuity as a Beast of Greed, until little by little a certain section of public opinion became infected by the poison. Journals of similar tendencies elsewhere in the country followed the lead with less ability and malignancy but with similar persistence. … As the scope of his political activity increased, the approbation which he wanted and needed had to come from a widely extended public opinion. Hence…he could not but wince under a personal distortion which was at once so gross and brutal, and yet so insidious and so impossible to combat…this concentration upon his own person of a class hatred and suspicion wounded and staggered him, until he became accustomed to it, and was better able to estimate its real effect upon public opinion."

Hearst profited from the attacks and their effectiveness, so much so that the post-election edition of the *Journal* broke all previous sales records by topping 1.5 million copies. He had owned the paper for barely a year.

Hearst is probably most famous – or infamous - for his involvement in getting the United States involved in the Spanish-American War. The Cuban Revolution of 1895 came at an ideal time for Hearst, who had just purchased the *Journal* and was looking for a way to make a name for himself on the East Coast. When the Cuban rebels declared their independence from Spain, their demands resonated with Hearst and many other Americans, and before long, the *Journal* was regularly promoting the rebels' cause by publishing articles and cartoons that portrayed the rebels as innocent victims of repeated atrocities by the Spanish.

Time and again, Hearst called upon the American government to intervene on behalf of the Cuban rebels, and he also made sure his reporters were always on the prowl for a scoop. They were even encouraged to become personally involved in events. In one of the most provocative stories of the era, reporter Karl Decker learned of a beautiful 17-year-old girl being held in a Spanish prison for supposedly inciting rebellion. Her name was Evangelina Cossio y Cisneros, and Decker was determined to obtain her freedom. He first tried to do so by bribing guards to let her out, and when that failed, he used his influence to persuade a Cuban dentist and an American businessman to break her out. The three took a ladder to the jail under the cover of darkness, climbed up to her window and managed to loosen enough bars in the decaying walls to free her. They spirited her away to the United States, where she gave the *Journal* exclusive access to her story.

Evangelina Cossio y Cisneros

In situations like these, rumors crop up that often last for generations. One of these involved a message that Hearst supposedly sent the famed artist Frederick Remington, who was then working for him as an illustrator. Hearst had sent Remington to Cuba to cover the fighting, but Remington cabled back to him that there was no fighting to cover, and that he wanted to return to America. According to legend, Hearst cabled back, "You furnish the pictures. I'll furnish the war."

W. Joseph Campbell, author of *Yellow Journalism: Puncturing the Myths, Defining the Legacies*, has questioned whether this actually happened, writing, "Reasons for doubting [James] Creelman's anecdote are many. They go beyond Hearst's denial, made in 1907 and repeated in the autobiography of one of his sons. They go beyond the fact that the telegrams Creelman described have never surfaced. … Searches of Remington's papers produced no reference to his purported exchange with Hearst. But the correspondence of Davis, the most prominent American war reporter of the time, offers telling evidence that the exchange never happened. In one letter, Davis said Remington left because he had 'all the material he needs for sketches and for illustrating my stories.' In a more expansive letter, Davis said he asked Remington to leave because Davis disliked 'traveling in pairs.'"

According to a 1998 *New York Times* article, "Many of the reporters who covered the Cuban uprising had front-page ink on their minds, not ethics…Hearst even sent a ceremonial sword with a diamond-studded ivory handle as a gift to General Maximo Gomez, commander of the Cuban rebel forces. An intrepid cub reporter, Ralph D. Paine, volunteered to present the sword to the rebel leader to get his first big scoop." Even those who were trying to keep clear of the drama often found themselves caught up in the media frenzy, as the *Times* noted in relaying the story of the well-respected foreign correspondent Richard Harding Davis: "Unwilling to get caught up in the hype, he left Cuba on the mail steamer Olivette without asking permission from his editors at The *Journal*. While steaming home, he met a young Cuban woman named Clemencia Arango, who was expelled by General Weyler as a suspected guerrilla collaborator. She told Mr. Davis that she had been repeatedly disrobed on the orders of Spanish detectives searching for secret messages to Cuban exiles in Tampa. Mr. Davis wrote about the woman's ordeal, but buried it in a longer piece. When his editors got down to the undressing part they saw red meat, and had Mr. Remington draw an illustration of a young woman, her naked rear end showing, forced to strip before Spanish agents. The *Journal's* headline read: 'Does Our Flag Shield Women?'" The article concluded, "Reporters following up on the story later learned that the Spanish agents had used matrons to do the undressing, and, as proper gentlemen, they never viewed the woman's naked body themselves. No matter; she became a cause celebre for the war hawks."

Remington

Davis

Despite leaders hoping to stay above the fray, American economic interests were being harmed by the ongoing conflict between Cuban nationalists and Spain, as merchants' trading with Cuba was suffering now that the island was undergoing conflict. Furthermore, the American press capitalized on the ongoing Cuban struggle for independence, which had been flaring up time and again since 1868. In an effort to sell papers, the press frequently sensationalized stories, which came to be known as yellow journalism, and during the run-up to war, yellow journalism spread false stories about the Cuban conflict in order to sell newspapers in the competitive New York City market.

President McKinley's wished to avoid a war, but he was forced to support a war with Spain after the USS *Maine* suffered an explosion in Havana's harbor in February 1898. McKinley had sent the ship to help protect American citizens in Cuba from the violence that was taking place there, but an explosion rocked the ship, which had to be towed to harbor and eventually scuttled. That took place only after 266 American sailors aboard the ship were killed.

No sooner had the men landed on American soil in Key West than they were besieged by questions about what they believed had happened on their ship. To their credit, most were reticent and discreet in their speculations. John Blandin noted, "I have no theories as to the cause of the explosion. I cannot form any. I, with others, had heard the Havana harbor was full of torpedoes [mines], but the officers whose duty it was to examine into that reported that they found no signs of any. Personally, I do not believe that the Spanish had anything to do with the disaster. Time may tell. I hope so. We were in a delicate position on the *Maine*, so far as taking any precautions was concerned. We were friends in a friendly, or alleged friendly port and could not fire upon or challenge the approach of any boat boarding us unless convinced that her intention was hostile. I wish to heaven I could forget it. I have been in two wrecks and have had my share. But the reverberations of that sullen, yet resonant roar, as if the bottom of the sea was groaning in torture, will haunt me for many days, and in the reflection of that pillar of flame comes to me even when I close my eyes."

Within just a few days of the explosion, American divers arrived to explore the ship's wreckage and file a report on what they saw. They were also there to try to recover as many bodies as they could. One recalled, "It was horrible!…As I descended into the death-ship the dead rose up to meet me. They floated toward me with outstretched arms, as if to welcome their shipmate. Their faces for the most part were bloated with decay or burned beyond recognition, but here and there the light of my lamp flashed upon a stony face I knew, which when I last saw it had smiled a merry greeting, but now returned my gaze with staring eyes and fallen jaw. The dead choked the hatchways and blocked my passage from stateroom to cabin. I had to elbow my way through them, as you do in a crowd. While I examined twisted iron and broken timbers they brushed against my helmet and touched my shoulders with rigid hands, as if they sought to tell me the tale of the disaster. I often had to push them aside to make my examinations of the interior of the wreck. I felt like a live man in command of the dead. From every part of the ship came sighs and groans. I knew it was the gurgling of the water through the shattered beams and battered sides of the vessel, but it made me shudder; it sounded so much like echoes of that awful February night of death. The water swayed the bodies to and fro, and kept them constantly moving with a hideous semblance of life. Turn which way I would, I was confronted by a corpse."

Photo # NH 46774 Diving on MAINE's wreck

Less than a month after the *Maine* went down, the United States Navy convened a board of inquiry to determine the cause of the explosion. Other than some sort of outside attack, the only other explanation, given the strength and location of the blast, was that some sort of fire broke out on the ship and detonated something flammable.

While authorities were trying to investigate the causes, New York's papers immediately tried to get out in front of each other with wildly speculative accounts, all of which blamed the Spanish. As Jim Squires noted, "Press responsibility was a big issue then, too. Pulitzer and his imitator/rival, William Randolph Hearst, were accused of starting the Spanish-American War with their unsupported and arguably irresponsible accusations that Spain had blown up the U.S. battleship Maine in Havana harbor. And the sleaziness of their juvenile public feud over a comic strip character called 'the Yellow Kid' spawned the infamous term 'yellow journalism,' which still lives today. Meanwhile, circulation doubled at Pulitzer's *World* to 800,000, tripled at Hearst's fledgling *Journal*, and newspapers in general were soon transformed from a small, elitist enterprise appealing to commercial and political interests to a medium for the masses. For the first time, immigrants had to learn how to read English just to get by."

A picture of the headline in the *New York World*, which belied the fact that Pulitzer privately conceded "nobody outside a lunatic asylum" should believe Spain was responsible.

The headline in William Randolph Hearst's *New York Journal*

Over 115 years later, the explosion of the *Maine* is perhaps best remembered for being associated with yellow journalism and as the primary cause of the Spanish-American War, which makes it somewhat fitting that the explosion itself remains an unsolved mystery. There was never another official public investigation carried out by the American government after 1911, but several private investigations have sought to answer the enduring mystery, and the most recent efforts have theorized that the explosion was an accident caused by burning coal. A 1974 investigation led by Admiral Hyman G. Rickover was the first major study to suggest that a spontaneous combustion of coal in one of the ship's bunkers triggered the explosion of an adjacent magazine, which then caused the heavy majority of the damage.

Ultimately, the loss of the USS *Maine* drew America into the war, and in that endeavor, McKinley and the federal government were given a shove from Hearst. As the *Times* noted a century later, "The first story in Pulitzer's New York World carried a banner headline that left little doubt about who was responsible: 'Maine Explosion Caused by Bomb or Torpedo?' The Journal published a diagram of what it called a secret 'infernal machine' that struck the ship like a deadly torpedo -- apparently the figment of some journalist's imagination."

When the United States finally declared war in 1898, Hearst personally traveled to Cuba to get a front row seat for the fighting. Chartering a yacht to live on while he was there, he ran the "Cuban Edition" of the *Journal*, making sure that his readers learned of extra gory detail of the battles, especially of any stories glorifying the rebels or vilifying the Spanish.

To be fair, Hearst was not merely out to sell newspapers; he did, in fact, believe in that the Cuban rebels were justified in their struggles. Spain had indeed been cruel in its treatment of the Cubans, and had executed hundreds of thousands of those who opposed them. Like Pulitzer, Hearst knew his audience well, and he never doubted that his readers would respond to the stories he told of these injustices. Those men covering the war for Hearst knew the importance of getting their stories, and two of them, Edward Marshall and James Creelman, were injured during the fighting. When the war was finished, General Calixto Garcia, the head of the Cuban rebels, presented Hearst with a bullet-riddled flag in recognition of his support for the rebel cause.

The war only lasted a few months, but it was long enough for Hearst to get a sense of his power in the nation, and he was not about to back down from telling the government what it ought to do. He continued to be a man whom politicians were wise to fear, for the *Morning Journal* was selling more than a million issues a day by the time the Spanish-American War started. In spite of this, Hearst continued to lose money on his publishing venture, perhaps as much as $1 million a year in his first few years in business. This was because, while he was selling plenty of papers, his prices were too low, so that he could continue to undercut Pulitzer. However, with the war over, the men were able to call a truce, and the *World* and the *Journal* stopped actively competing with each other in 1898.

Pulitzer's Final Years

"Don't be sensitive if I should, in future, seem brusque, harsh, or even unjust in my criticism. I sincerely hope I never shall be; but if I should, remember that fault-finding is perhaps both my privilege and my weakness, that correction is the only road to improvement, and that my quick temper and illness are entitled to some consideration." – Joseph Pulitzer

Pulitzer seemed repentant in the years following the war, and he began to steer away from some of the most lurid stories, focusing instead on political issues and uncovering graft in politics. This gain him the respect of many, and as he grew older, he was frequently asked for interviews. He rarely agreed, but when he did, he enjoyed speaking out about the current state of journalism in America. In a May 1904 article in *The North American Review*, Pulitzer declared, "Our Republic and its press will rise or fall together. An able, disinterested, public-spirited press, with trained intelligence to know the right and courage to do it, can preserve that public virtue without which popular government is a sham and a mockery. A cynical, mercenary, demagogic press will produce in time a people as base as itself. The power to mould the future of the Republic will be in the hands of the journalists of future generations." Indeed, he was notoriously supportive of the work his reporters did; it was the editors of the paper that found him nearly unbearable to work for. When asked why this was so, he replied with one of his most famous quotes: "Because a reporter is always a hope and an editor always a disappointment."

In 1904, Pulitzer made one of the most important and trying decisions of his life when he hired Frank Cobb as editor of the *World*. While his previous editors had been somewhat in awe of the legendary publisher, Cobb was more inclined to stand up to him and even challenge Pulitzer's decisions, especially when they concerned what he perceived to be attempts to micromanage his work. On more than one occasion, those listening outside would hear screaming matches between the two men, with each apparently trying to outdo the other with profanity. Not only did they disagree about internal policies, they also argued over world events, and which side of political issues the *World* should support.

Cobb

It was their commitment to excellence in journalism, and to Woodrow Wilson's campaign, that gave them common ground to work with, but there was one particularly explosive moment between them. Decades later, historian Louis Starr described what happened: "On April 10, 1907, his sixtieth birthday, Pulitzer resigned as president of his two publishing companies, in St. Louis and New York, in favor of his eldest son, Ralph. From his retreat on the Riviera he cabled a farewell message which, while designed to be read at employees' dinners in the two cities, embodied a stirring statement of his philosophy of journalism and was clearly addressed to the world at large. He had polished it for days. In St. Louis, the *Post-Dispatch* printed it—and indeed continues to print it in capital letters under its masthead on the editorial page. In New York, other papers published the message, but not the *World*. Cobb would have none of it. J. P. had already resigned as editor of the *World* in another ringing statement back in 1890, early in his invalidism. One resignation was enough. Besides, Cobb knew better than anyone that Joseph Pulitzer could not for the life of him resign in any meaningful sense as long as he breathed. Why pretend? The blind man fairly howled with rage, but the deed was done. Cobb would run the message in his own way, and in his own good time."

Ironically, the most quoted and memorable part of Pulitzer's resignation read, "I know that my retirement will make no difference in its cardinal principles; that it will always fight for progress and reform, never tolerate injustice or corruption, always fight demagogues of all parties, never belong to any party, always oppose privileged classes and public plunderers, never lack sympathy with the poor, always remain devoted to the public welfare, never be satisfied with merely printing news, always be drastically independent, never be afraid to attack wrong…"

In spite of these many controversies, or perhaps because of them, Pulitzer seems to have held a secret respect for Cobb, and he worked with Cobb to solidify some of the *World*'s editorial policies. This pleased Cobb, who wrote to Pulitzer on May 9, 1908, "Four years ago today, I began work on the World. You will believe me, I know, when I say I would not barter these four years for any other years of my life."

Starr noted of this correspondence, "Pulitzer did believe him, for by now he knew his man. In December of that year, the two held a long skull session aboard J. P.'s new ocean-going hospital, the colossal steam yacht Liberty, off New York Harbor. Cobb's long memorandum of the conversation shows the forever dissatisfied one insisting that 'the news treatment of politics and allied subjects must be raised, in temper, tone, accuracy, restraint, and moral courage, to the level… [of] the editorial columns.' Accordingly, Pulitzer outlined an experimental plan to make Cobb his overseer of both the news and editorial departments, 'to the end that Mr. P.'s principles of journalism shall be…indelibly stamped upon the news columns…and that if possible the Pulitzer tradition shall remain with the World long after Mr. Pulitzer and also Mr. Cobb are dead.' The scheme never quite materialized, but it suggests the publisher's esteem for Cobb. 'The Page' was enough for Cobb. 'You once said that there was more joy in making an editorial page than in anything else you knew of,' he wrote Pulitzer in 1910. 'I fully agree with you.'"

For his part, Pulitzer planned to spend most of his remaining time on the yacht he had just purchased. One historian from Columbia University later mused, "Perhaps the only place on earth where Joseph Pulitzer was truly happy following the loss of his sight was at sea on his beautiful yacht the 'Liberty.' Built for him by the Ramage and Ferguson shipyard of Leith, Scotland, for $1.5 million, the 300-foot yacht was christened in December, 1907. It was specially designed to minimize all noise, from the bulkhead to every door and porthole. In it, Pulitzer was able to travel around the globe in a cocoon of silence, served by a forty-five man crew, and a twelve-man staff of personal assistants to read aloud, play music, or provide conversation."

However, true to form, Pulitzer could not resist meddling in politics, especially when it involved accusing a Republican administration of misdeeds. In 1909, the *World* ran a story claiming that a payment of $40 million made by the federal government to the French Panama Canal Company was fraudulent. Furious, President Theodore Roosevelt fought back by ordering the federal government to indict Pulitzer for libeling him and the powerful banker, J.P. Morgan. Instead of backing off the investigation and issuing an apology, Pulitzer forged ahead, bringing his investigation to its conclusion. The courts dismissed the charges filed against him and the paper, handing a significant victory to the principle of freedom of the press.

Pulitzer became increasingly philosophical toward the end of his life, and this made him more of an open book for those who wished to know what had shaped his life and work. He was constantly asked about his life decisions, and the attitudes that drove them. In 1911, he wrote to someone, "Every issue of the paper presents an opportunity and a duty to say something courageous and true; to rise above the mediocre and conventional; to say something that will command the respect of the intelligent, the educated, the independent part of the community; to rise above fear of partisanship and fear of popular prejudice. I would rather have one article a day of this sort; and these ten or twenty lines might readily represent a whole day's hard work in the way of concentrated, intense thinking and revision, polish of style, weighing of words."

Just months later, while traveling to his home on Jekyll Island in Georgia in October 1911, Pulitzer fell ill. Concerned about his already precarious health, his staff docked his yacht in Charleston, South Carolina. Seeing that there was nothing more he could do, his personal physician, Dr. Guthman, who was traveling with him, told Pulitzer's son, Herbert, who was also with them, to contact Kate and have her to come immediately to join them. She arrived in time to be with her husband at the end.

According to his obituary, Pulitzer "died aboard his yacht, the Liberty, in Charleston Harbor at 1:40 o'clock this afternoon (October 29). The immediate cause of Mr. Pulitzer's death was heart disease. Although he had been in poor health for some time, there was no suspicion on the part of those accompanying him that his condition was serious. … The change for the worse came at about 2 o'clock this morning, when he suffered an attack of severe pain. By daylight he appeared to be better and fell asleep soon after 10:30. He awoke at 1 o'clock and complained of pain in his heart. Soon he fell into a faint and expired at 1:40 o'clock."

Fittingly, Pulitzer died with a newspaper in his hand. "Up to an hour and a half before his death Mr. Pulitzer's mind remained perfectly clear. His German secretary had been reading to him an account of the reign of Louis the Eleventh of France, in whose career Mr. Pulitzer had always taken the liveliest interest. As the secretary neared the end of his chapter and came to the death of the French King, Mr. Pulitzer said to him: 'Leise, ganz leise, ganz leise.' (softly, quite softly.) These were the last words he spoke."

Pulitzer's will revealed a pleasant surprise for New York's Columbia University, as he had left $2 million to that institution to endow a School of Journalism. He explained the decision, writing, "I am deeply interested in the progress and elevation of journalism, having spent my life in that profession, regarding it as a noble profession and one of unequalled importance for its influence upon the minds and morals of the people. I desire to assist in attracting to this profession young men of character and ability, also to help those already engaged in the profession to acquire the highest moral and intellectual training. There are now special schools for instruction for lawyers, physicians, clergymen, military and naval officers, engineers, architects and artists, but none for the instruction of journalists. That all other professions and not journalism should have the advantage of special training seems to me contrary to reason. I have felt that I could contribute in no more effectual way to the benefit of my profession and to the public good than by providing for founding and maintaining adequate schools of journalism."

Of course, the most significant clause in Pulitzer's will related to the prizes he wished to be given in his name to those who exhibited excellence in journalism. Pulitzer Prize historian Seymour Topping explained, "Pulitzer specified solely four awards in journalism, four in letters and drama, one for education, and five traveling scholarships. ... In journalism, prizes were to recognize 'the most disinterested and meritorious public service rendered by any American newspaper during the preceding year'...'the best editorial article written during the year, the test of excellence being clearness of style, moral purpose, sound reasoning, and power to influence public opinion in the right direction'...and the best example of a reporter's work during the year, the test being strict accuracy, terseness, the accomplishment of some public good commanding public attention and respect.... In letters, prizes were to go to an American novel..., an original American play performed in New York..., a book on the history of the United States...and an American biography...."

Knowing from personal experience how much times could change over the years, Pulitzer's will stipulated that an "Advisory Board shall have power in its discretion to suspend or to change any subject or subjects, substituting, however, others in their places, if in the judgment of the Board such suspension, changes or substitutions shall be conducive to the public good or rendered advisable by public necessities or by reason of change of time. It is my intention that all the sums herein before specified for prizes shall be used for prizes only, and for no other purpose whatsoever."

Thus, in death as in life, Joseph Pulitzer ensured he would continue to have a profound impact on journalism, and the world at large.

New Pursuits

No longer focused entirely on beating out Pulitzer in New York, Hearst was able to expand his interests nationally. In the early years of the 20th century, he established newspapers in cities as diverse as Boston and Los Angeles, as well as Chicago. Hearst biographers Oliver Carlson and Ernest Sutherland Bates, writing in the mid-1930s, explained some of the hardships these maneuvers entailed: "The establishment of a new paper in Chicago was not an easy matter in those days, especially when the invader was as dangerous as Hearst was recognized to be. The rival papers hired thugs to run his newsboys off the streets. But such methods were not likely to terrorize an heir of the San Francisco vigilantes. Hearst hired more thugs than his enemies and ran their newsboys off the streets. When thug met thug, a fine battle would ensue. Teamsters and delivery men joined the holy war on behalf of their masters, until traffic became so disrupted that the police at last interfered to restore law and order. It was evident that Hearst had come to stay. How well he had mastered the methodology for such crises was shown years later when the Hearst papers in San Francisco employed identically the same means to keep Cornelius Vanderbilt out of their field."

Hearst also remained heavily involved in national politics, regularly denouncing President William McKinley, in his editorials, including one in which he declared, "If bad institutions and bad men can be got rid of only by killing, then the killing must be done." He quickly regretted using such harsh language and dispatched Creelman to the White House to make amends. According to Creelman, "Mr. Hearst offered to exclude from his papers anything that the President might find personally offensive. Also he pledged the President hearty support in all things as to which Mr. Hearst did not differ with him politically. The President seemed deeply touched by this wholly voluntary offer and sent a message of sincere thanks."

Creelman

McKinley

Despite the olive branch, Hearst soon resumed his attacks on McKinley, and when McKinley was assassinated shortly after being reelected, many in the nation were incensed. In fact, some subsequently asserted without any evidence that Hearst's writing had inspired the assassin. Following McKinley's death on September 14, 1901, the Grand Army of the Republic, still held in the highest esteem for the Civil War, resolved, "That every member of the Grand Army of the Republic exclude from his household 'The New York Journal,' a teacher of anarchism and a vile sheet, unfit for perusal by any one who is a respecter of morality and good government."

McKinley's successor, President Theodore Roosevelt, also took up the cry. During his first message to Congress in December 1901, he insisted, "When we turn from the man to the Nation, the harm done is so great as to excite our gravest apprehensions and to demand our wisest and most resolute action. This criminal was a professed anarchist, inflamed by the teachings of professed anarchists, and probably also by the reckless utterances of those who, on the stump and in the public press, appeal to the dark and evil spirits of malice and greed, envy and sullen hatred. The wind is sowed by the men who preach such doctrines, and they cannot escape their share of responsibility for the whirlwind that is reaped. This applies alike to the deliberate demagogue, to the exploiter of sensationalism, and to the crude and foolish visionary who, for whatever reason, apologizes for crime or excites aimless discontent."

In an attempt to mitigate at least some of the considerable damage done to his reputation and that of his paper, Hearst changed the name of the *Morning Journal* to the *American* after McKinley's death. He also considered running for public office himself, no doubt hoping to punish Roosevelt for his cutting words. In public, of course, he cast running for office as a moral, civic duty, claiming, "My early ambition was to do my part in newspapers, and I still propose to do a newspaper part. But when I saw mayors and governors and presidents fall, I felt that I'd like to see if I couldn't do better. I felt I'd like to go into office, any office almost, to see if I couldn't do the things I wanted to see done." According to Carlson and Bates, what Hearst really believed was that a "political office, any office almost, could be a stepping-stone to the presidency, but that some political office was a prerequisite."

Thus, Hearst set about on his own political career. Carlson and Bates explained, "Hearst chose the easiest and most available, that of representative from the Eleventh Congressional District of the City of New York, an office entirely under the control of Charles F. Murphy, the reigning boss of Tammany Hall. The publisher's decision to enter politics was opposed by most of his friends. There was still a journalistic tradition, more honored in the breach than the observance, that an editor should be independent of political parties, and should never sacrifice this independence by becoming a candidate for office. The experience of the one prominent journalist who had gone into politics, Horace Greeley, vainly seeking the presidency and dying of chagrin after his defeat, was not such as to encourage imitation. But Hearst knew that he should not die, and his determination remained unshaken."

Hearst launched his campaign on October 6, 1902, telling an audience gathered to hear his first political speech, "I believe that of the eighty millions of people in this country, five or six millions (the most prosperous five or six millions) are ably represented in Congress, in the law courts, and in the newspapers. It would be immodesty on my part to imagine that I could add much to the comfort or prosperity of the few who are so thoroughly well looked after. My ambition is to forward the interests of the seventy millions or more of typical Americans who are not so well looked after. Their needs seem to offer a wider field for useful effort. At the same time let me say that I do not seek to divide the nation into classes or foster unreasoning dislike of one class by another. I can recognize and admire the genius and the generosity of the great captains of industry…My interest is in the average American citizen. The welfare of the country demands that he too shall secure a fair share in the advantages of prosperity…" Hearst won his election easily.

Now nearly 40 years old, Hearst decided to get married and settle down. However, much to the chagrin of his closest friends, he eschewed the many suitable daughters of New York society and instead married a 21-year-old vaudeville dancer named Millicent Willson. The two were married on April 28, 1903 and immediately left for an extended honeymoon in Europe.

Millicent Hearst

These were hardly the actions of a committed politician, but then, there was nothing to suggest Hearst was all that committed to his political career. In fact, Carlson and Bates noted, "No congressman ever took his legislative duties more lightly than did Congressman Hearst. He rarely attended the meetings of the House, and when he did, he voted still more rarely. During the first and second sessions of the Fifty-Eighth Congress, which were continuous from November 9, 1903, to April 28, 1904, he responded to the roll-call but nine times."

With that said, Hearst did champion a handful of bills, including the following list:

"an amendment to the Interstate Commerce Act, giving the Interstate Commerce Commission the power to fix railroad rates;

an amendment to the Sherman Anti-Trust Act designed to strengthen it;

an inquiry relative to alleged railroad combinations in the transportation of anthracite coal;

a bill to appoint a committee for the investigation of trusts;

one to establish a parcel post system; another to regulate towing at sea."

As Carlson and Bates concluded, "All of these were enlightened measures…And, once having introduced his resolutions and seen them referred to the appropriate committees, where nearly all died a natural death, Hearst took no further interest in them save to give the impression through his newspapers that he was an exceedingly active congressman."

In spite of his relatively paltry record and lax participation, Hearst won reelection. He ran for the presidency in 1904, but he was unable to secure the Democratic nomination. After that, he turned his sights to the New York City mayoral race in 1905, which he lost. He then lost his bid to become New York's governor in 1906. He ran for mayor again in 1907, this time as a member of the Municipal Ownership League, a political party he established himself. He lost again.

When Hearst ran for mayor again in 1909, the whole thing had become something of a running joke. As one writer not so delicately put it, "During the ten years William has been active in New York State politics, he has been identified with more parties as a candidate or a promoter of candidates of his own personal selection than any other man in fifty years. At one time or another he has been the regular party candidate of two parties — the Democratic and Independence League, or Independence party, as it later became known. He has openly fused with the Republicans on two occasions, once in promoting the candidacy for sheriff of Max F. Ihmsen, his campaign manager for several years, and with the Republican organization then in control of former Governor Odell in 1903 to elect. He has been active in both the major political parties and has twice operated a party of his own. He has frequently been a candidate for office; with the exception of one inconspicuous term in the lower House of Congress, these ambitions have not met with success at the polls anti-Tammany candidates to the board of aldermen. In the present campaign he has fused with the Republicans to the extent of hitching on to all the candidates nominated by the regular Republican organization with the exception of mayor."

Perhaps not surprisingly, Hearst's experiences led to his disenchantment with politics. Looking for something new to excite his interest, he spent the next several years expanding his business empire. Already owning a number of newspapers, Hearst purchased two news services, and he molded one of them into the *International News Services* in 1909. Decades later, it would merge with the *United Press* to become the now famous *United Press International*.

During this period in his life, Hearst joined many other men of his age and station in becoming fascinated by the emerging aviation industry. It all began in January 1909, when a French pilot, Louis Paulhan, took him up on his first flight. In an article published on January 22, 1910 in *The Editor and Publisher*, Hearst breathlessly described the experience, writing, "We left the commonplace of this worn-out world behind us, beneath us, and lifted into a new life, into a new era. The sensations of flying are difficult to describe, for the human mind operates through analogy and is convinced by comparisons, and there is nothing with which to compare the sensations of flying. I felt that great sense of exhilaration which all aviators describe, and in addition a deep serenity, a calm enjoyment of what seemed to be the perfect conditions of a new and better state. The little people below, growing littler, too, every moment, seemed to belong to the past, to a period when men walked miserably upon the face of the earth or rolled uncomfortably in primitive autos over the rough surface. We…were of the new era; we were soaring gloriously through space; we were flying. As a matter of fact, M. Paulhan was doing the flying and I was merely holding on. and quite tight, too, but I felt altogether as grand and superior as he could possibly have felt."

In 1910, Hearst established the Hearst Transcontinental Prize of $50,000 (more than $1 million today) to be given to the first pilot to fly from one coast to another in fewer than 30 days. No one managed to accomplish this feat before the prize expired in November 1911, but in the years that followed, he sponsored *Old Glory*, a Fokker F.Vlla single-engine monoplane, in a failed attempt to cross the Atlantic. It would take more than another decade for Charles Lindbergh to accomplish that feat.

While maturity moved Hearst away from sensationalizing stories, he never lost his boyish interest in cartoons, and throughout his career he hired and promoted some of the most talented artists of the era. Among them was George Herriman, who in 1913 invented a strip called *Krazy Kat*. While it initially made only a minimal stir in the publishing world, Hearst stood by it and kept it running for decades, insisting it was a classic. It was only after the comic ended in 1944 that many critics acknowledged he was right.

Herriman

A *Krazy Kat* cartoon

Anxious to consolidate and protect the copyrights of his popular comic strips, in 1914 Heart founded King Features Syndicate as a single corporation owning all his syndicated features. Within two years, King Features had carved a niche for itself in the newspaper business, bringing on staff members to create and draw new material that it could in turn sell to newspapers across America. During the years of the Great Depression, the company provided features to more than 13,700 newspapers.

Politically, Hearst remained a populist, but he became steadily more interested in isolationism than in any other issue. In a 2016 article for *The Atlantic*, writer Eric Rauchway spelled out some of Hearst's activities and stances during World War I: "Before the United States entered World War I, Hearst's sympathies lay with Germany. He used his publishing empire to gather pro-German editors and writers around him, did a deal with a German agent for newsreel footage, and used a paid agent of the German government as his newspaper correspondent for German matters. But once the United States declared war on Germany, Hearst could no longer maintain this stance, so he took up a new one. With American flags decorating his newspapers' masthead, he declared that the freshly belligerent Americans should tender no aid to the Allies also fighting Germany: '[K]eep every dollar and every man and every weapon and all our supplies and stores AT HOME, for the defense of our own land, our own people, our own freedom, until that defense has been made ABSOLUTELY secure. After that we can think of other nations' troubles. But till then, America first!' Wilson had used 'America first' to position the United States as an international leader; Hearst interpreted the slogan to mean preserving, in sympathy with the Germans, above all and absolutely the security of the American homeland and the American people. Hearst's version stuck, not least because he revived it to oppose the 1932 nomination of Franklin Roosevelt for president and to invent the candidacy of John Nance Garner." Hearst remained pro-German and anti-Wilson in the years following the war, and he stringently opposed the president's vision for the League of Nations.

Already enamored with the burgeoning movie business, in 1915 Hearst established an animation studio called the International Film Service. Animation was an easy business to break into for Hearst since he already owned many of the most popular comic strips in the United States. A few years later, in 1918, he partnered with Paramount tycoon Adolph Zukor to form Cosmopolitan Pictures in New York City. The deal benefitted both men, as Zukor was given first refusal for the rights to make movies from stories featured in Hearst's many magazines. At the same time, the members of the public who had already read the stories or merely heard of them were essentially a preexisting audience that would likely be anxious to see the film. Naturally, the Hearst magazines would help with promotion by publishing articles that publicized the movies.

The King of His Castles

What most Americans did not know (and most likely would not want to know) was that Hearst's reasons for creating Cosmopolitan Pictures were at least as personal as they were practical. Now in his early 50s, Hearst appeared to be a devoted husband and proud father of five growing sons: George Randolph, born in 1904; William Randolph, Jr., born in 1908; John Randolph, 1910; and twins Randolph Apperson and David Whitmire, born in 1915. However, the supposedly settled businessman had fallen in love with a 20-year-old showgirl named Marion Davies.

Unlike most relationships involving married men and mistresses in the early 20ᵗʰ century,

Hearst was devoted to Davies from the start, and he remained committed to her for the rest of his life. She wanted a career in movies, so he created a movie studio that would cast her without any questions. Writing for *Slate* magazine in 2015, Karina Longworth explained, "In 1918 Hearst signed Davies to a contract with his newly-formed production company, Cosmopolitan Pictures, at $5 a week. Davies had a stutter, but that didn't matter—she had big, expressive eyes, highly photogenic blonde hair, and an adorable pout. Even Davies' detractors would have to admit that she was incredibly photogenic, and she could sell a joke. Davies' memoirs reveal the actress to have a dry sense of humor, above all about herself. As she would crack about her career beginnings, 'I couldn't act, but the idea of silent pictures appealed to me because I couldn't talk either.' Hearst's stroke of genius when it came to Marion Davies was to use what he had already proven had worked…If he wanted something to happen, he would report that it was happening, and then it would happen. And so Hearst put the weight of his newspaper empire into spreading the news about this amazing new star, Marion Davies, and then he found some movies for her to star in. By 1920, Davies had appeared in seven films…"

Marion Davies

As a wealthy man with both a wife and a mistress, Hearst believed he needed a new home where he and Davies could live together, away from disapproving eyes. To this end, in 1919, he began work on what would come to be known as Hearst Castle. Located on his ranch near San Simeon, California, which sprawled across over 240,000 acres, Hearst Castle would become the center of life and entertainment for many celebrities on the West Coast in the years to come.

Historian Jana Seely offered a virtual tour of what guests could expect at Hearst Castle: "All the guests at San Simeon occupied rooms furnished with the works of art accumulated by Hearst. They slept in sixteenth-century beds, kept their clothes in seventeenth-century chests of drawers, and watched fires burning beneath five-hundred-year-old mantels…One of the ways William Randolph Hearst ensured others' enjoyment of art was by enlivening mundane domestic items with antique components. Hearst residences were furnished not only with fine antique mantels, but also with antique fireplace equipment such as andirons, pokers and grates. Wrought-iron candlestands were transformed into floor lamps, marble columns were used as sculpture pedestals, iron grilles protected windows, and architectural elements such as ceilings were frequently incorporated into the very fabric of the building, often augmented, sometimes altered, by the work of Hearst craftsmen…This intense interest in a wide range of objects not traditionally sought by the other great collectors is one of the factors that sets William Randolph Hearst apart and contributes to his reputation as something of a maverick. His purchases included doorknockers, warming pans, tile stoves, musical instruments, pipes, and lanterns in addition to mainstream art such as paintings, sculpture, tapestries and silver."

Needless to say, everyone wanted to be invited to "the Ranch," as Hearst called it, and during the 1920s and 1930s, he and Davies hosted one decadent weekend party after another. Hearst made sure that the estate was always easy for his guests to reach, even those who could not fly in in their own planes and land at the estate's on site airstrip. For these less fortunate guests, Hearst provided a private train car that they could take from Los Angeles. Those arriving were typically left to their own designs during the day, but at night they could expect to meet anyone from Clark Gable to Winston Churchill around the dinner table. Franklin D. Roosevelt stayed over early in his career, as did Bob Hope and Cary Grant. Charlie Chaplin might be seen complaining about the impact of talking pictures on the movie industry, while Charles Lindbergh praised the rising Third Reich. After dinner, guests were often invited to view a first run movie, from Cosmopolitan Studios, of course, in the estate's private theater.

A picture of Hearst Castle

One of Hearst Castle's guest houses

Bernard Gagnon's picture of the Hearst Castle dining room

For times when he did not wish to entertain, or to do so in an even more private setting, Hearst could retreat to his estate on the McCloud River in Siskiyou County, California. Called Wyntoon after a local group of Native Americans, it had been built by his mother in 1902. So enamored was Hearst of the Bavarian style mansion that he used the same architect, Julia Morgan, to design Hearst Castle. However, Phoebe did not leave the estate to Hearst when she died in 1919, instead willing it to her favorite niece, Anne Flint. Determined not to lose the home his family had enjoyed for years, Hearst immediately began to scheme to get the property back, and in 1925 he purchased it from Flint for just under $200,000.

Hearst was acquiring everything he wanted, and he was bearing the brunt of the publicity surrounding his relationship with Davies, but that still had ramifications for everyone else involved. Longworth observed, "it was common knowledge that Davies was Hearst's mistress. … The Catholic Hearst hadn't divorced his wife, Millicent, and he never would—but Davies would live with Hearst openly for decades." This all but ensured nobody would take Davies' movies seriously, though Longworth pointed out that Davies was actually "fun, funny, and liked by just about everyone, and other papers were starting to take notice of Davies' beauty and vitality, particularly after the 1921 film Enchantment, in which Davies played a flapper a full two years before…the flapper type's on-screen debut."

Davies in *When Knighthood Was in Flower* (1922)

Ironically, Hearst disapproved of such vapid roles, determined that this modern girl he was living with should behave off stage in the same manner in which his wife and mother conducted themselves. As Longworth noted, many believed "it was exactly their non-conventional relationship that made Hearst so intent on protecting Davies' persona. Hearst knew he and Marion could never marry, and because of that he knew that she would always be considered by many to be a fallen woman, living in sin. In insisting that she never lose her quote-unquote dignity on screen, Hearst was in a sense trying to restore the virtue he had felt he had robbed from her in life."

Over the next few years, Hearst kept pouring virtually unlimited resources into Davies' career. Longworth continued, "In February 1923, Hearst found a distribution partner for his production company in Goldwyn Pictures. A little more than a year later…Goldwyn's assets were brought into [Metro-Goldwyn-Mayer], including…their contract with Hearst, which meant that Davies and her movies were now de facto property of MGM. Hearst went on to negotiate an unprecedented deal for himself and Marion, who he had named president of his Cosmopolitan

Pictures in order to ensure that she would get a sizable share of the profits, and have money of her own. Under the MGM deal, the studio fully financed the movies, and turned 30 percent of the profits over to Hearst and Davies, who was also paid a salary of $10,000 a week, of which MGM paid 60 percent and Hearst paid the rest…In exchange for financing and distributing Marion's movies, MGM had unlimited access to Hearst publications for the promotion of its films." This was an important consideration, and it likely smoothed Davies' way when it came to talking pictures, but no matter how much talent she had, her professional life was always overshadowed by her relationship with Hearst.

It was during this period that Hearst made one of his most unusual purchases in the form of St. Donat's Castle in Vale of Glamorgan, Wales. He first saw the property in an issue of *Country Life Magazine* in 1907 but never forgot it. Ultimately, he bought the castle in 1925 and began restoring it as a gift for Davies. Together, the two traveled throughout Europe, spending exorbitant sums to purchase entire rooms for themselves that they found in other castles. Hearst even bought the Great Hall, guest house, tithe barn and Prior's lodging from Bradenstoke Priory in England and had them dismantled and moved to St. Donat. He had the Great Hall completely rebuilt and used materials from the other buildings to create a banqueting hall at St. Donat's. Updating the structure, he added 34 bathrooms to accommodate the needs of his many guests. Each had fixtures made entirely of green and white marble.

Mick Lobb's picture of the castle from its courtyard

No matter what else he was doing, Hearst was always first and foremost a newspaper man, and while he was often dogmatic on issues concerning American politics, he was not so certain or committed when it came to his attitudes concerning other countries. In some cases, this worked to his credit, such as when he initially supported the Bolshevik Revolution when it began in Russia in 1917 but turned against the communists as the unrest and bloodshed spread. If there was any steadfast principle, it was that Hearst generally opposed American involvement in any overseas conflict, or even peacekeeping efforts, such as those proposed by Wilson for the League of Nations.

By the time the Roaring Twenties were in full spring, Hearst was one of the most influential men in America. He owned 28 newspapers across the country, from the *Seattle Post-Intelligencer* to the *Washington Times*, and he had also expanded his interests into publishing books and magazines, including such still popular periodicals as *Good Housekeeping* and *Harper's Bazaar*. His most controversial publication, however, was the *New York Daily Mirror*, a tabloid he launched in 1924. In the decade that followed, Hearst would have a mixed relationship with the broadsheet, selling it in 1928 and then buying it back in 1932.

In addition to promoting papers and movies, in the late 1920s Hearst also became more interested in air travel. In 1929, just months before the stock market crashed and he lost much of his fortune, Hearst spent a sizeable sum of money sponsoring the airship LZ 127 Graf Zeppelin on its famous voyage around the world. The voyage began at the Naval Air Station at Lakehurst, New Jersey, which would become known for being the site of the famous Hindenburg disaster. The ship returned to Lakehurst just three weeks later.

While he would likely never admit it, Hearst's fortune was never entirely his own, and at many turns, newspaper empire did not always break even. He had long been dependent for capital on the fortune his father had created, which meant the Great Depression drove many of his publications out of business. He made his losses worse by publicly opposing President Roosevelt's efforts to change the country's economic direction. Roosevelt was a popular man, and many of his supporters refused to buy papers that criticized him. Eric Rauchway noted, "Hearst…stepped forward in January [1932] with a speech decrying the internationalist Roosevelt as a Wilsonian meddler, opportunist, and the sort of fellow who would 'allow the international bankers and the other big influences that have gambled with your prosperity to gamble with your politics.' Hearst preferred 'a man … whose guiding motto is "'America First,'"." and named Garner—the Texas congressman who had, for slightly less than a month, been speaker of the House—as that man. Garner did not then know he was the leading anti-Roosevelt candidate for president or that, as an inveterate free-trader, his motto was 'America First.' Hearst, unfazed, hired a campaign biographer to invent a log-cabin birth and other suitable prerequisites for Garner, whose appeal, as one observer noted, was as 'a Democratic Coolidge'—or, as Garner himself said, someone who believed 'the gravest possible menace' facing the country was 'the constantly increasing tendency toward socialism and communism.' Here, he was reciting a verse from the Hearst hymnal."

Film historian Deborah Carmichael observed, "Hearst…brought his political message to millions of moviegoers in 1933 with his Cosmopolitan Films' production of "Gabriel Over the White House." Collaborating with scriptwriter Carey Wilson, Hearst himself wrote some of the politically charged oratory of President Hammond (Walter Houston). It is quickly revealed that President Hammond, a pleasure-loving and pliable politician, has gained the presidency through the support of party leaders. These leaders remind him regularly of the many favors he owes them. He answers to political shysters and not the American people suffering through the Great Depression. After a life-changing event…this fictional president experiences a spiritual and political epiphany guided by the archangel Gabriel…. A transformed President Hammond, who now resembles Abraham Lincoln physically and spiritually, acts rapidly to rid the nation of an unseen enemy--rum-running gangsters. Invoking his position as commander in chief, he adjourns Congress, disbands his Cabinet, institutes martial law, and after conviction by a military tribunal, orders death by firing squad in the shadow of the Statue of Liberty for the bootleggers who have threatened the stability of the country. Hammond further eliminates domestic problems by forming a CCC-like program. He gets foreign debts repaid by bullying world leaders with a display of military might. The problem of returning to a constitutional government is neatly solved as Gabriel, an angel of both vengeance and mercy, kills off President Hammond, who returns to his former self after completing the rescue of his country."

In a move he would come to regret, Hearst also started publishing articles written by the rising German leader Adolf Hitler. He praised Hitler for opposing the spread of communism and for focusing his attention on improving his own country. Hearst felt that Hitler's style of nationalism was something Americans could learn from, apparently seeing no problem with the fact that Hitler was notorious for encouraging his followers to beat up anyone who opposed the Nazis.

When Roosevelt won the Democratic nomination in 1932, Hearst used all the influence he could muster to force Roosevelt to choose John Nance Garner as his running mate. Pleased that Roosevelt did so, Hearst supported him in his run and for the first few months he was in office. However, Roosevelt's plans for the New Deal were too liberal and too radical for the son of a self-made millionaire, and Hearst ultimately went after him with all his might. Rauchway explained, "With 'AMERICA FIRST' at the center of his newspaper masthead, emblazoned above a stylized eagle clutching a ribbon reading, 'AN AMERICAN PAPER FOR THE AMERICAN PEOPLE,'…Hearst now saw communism everywhere—not only in the Roosevelt administration, but among college professors 'teaching alien doctrines' and among striking union workers in San Francisco, against whom Hearst's papers encouraged vigilante violence."

Once again, Hearst had seemingly changed his political stripes. According to biographer Ben Proctor,: "During the 1920s he became an avowed Jeffersonian Democrat, warning his fellow citizens against the dangers of big government, of unchecked federal power that could infringe on the individual rights of Americans, especially if a charismatic leader was in charge….[After supporting FDR in 1932] Hearst soon became highly critical of the New Deal. With increasing frequency Hearst newspapers supported big business to the detriment of organized labor. With unabated vigor they condemned higher income tax legislation as a persecution of the "successful.""

By 1937, Hearst was teetering on the edge of financial ruin. A quite unflattering article published on July 9 of that year told readers, "One by one reactionary newspapers are finding surcease in the journalistic boneyard—victims of the own publisher's personal hatred and stupidity. Two Hearst owned papers, the Rochester Herald and the New York American, recently have suspended publication. The American, for many years the most powerful paper in the Hearst chain, had been losing ground for several years and it known to have lost its owners a cool million last year." The article concluded sardonically, "Newspaper dictatorship, as exemplified by some of the metropolitan dailies, like political dictatorship, is bound to run its course. Sooner or later public opinion will make itself felt."

While some may have sympathy for Hearst's losses related to his political beliefs, he made plenty of business and personal mistakes that also contributed to his downfall. For one thing, he always had a difficult relationship with blue collar workers, and he often suffered at the hands of strikes organized by trade unions. He also failed to keep up with the changing times and fell behind new competitors, such as the *New York Daily News*, that thrived during this time. When money became tight, he refused to economize, instead purchasing more expensive art pieces for his collection and mortgaging San Simeon for $600,000 to pay for his lifestyle. When Joseph P. Kennedy, Sr. a rising millionaire, politician, and patriarch of the Kennedy political dynasty, offered to buy Hearst's magazines, he refused to sell.

Kennedy

On top of it all, Davies' film career was tanking, and most of the movies Hearst made lost money.

In an attempt to dig himself out of the financial hole he was in, Hearst eventually parted with an extensive part of his art collection. These sales are perhaps the only reason the public ever learned just how much money he had tied up in his collection. In 1937 alone, he sold off more than $11 million, which bought him some relief, but he still had to sell another 20,000 items, including paintings, chalices, croziers, windows and pulpits from ancient churches, a sideboard once owned by Charles Dickens, and Thomas Jefferson's Bible, as well as a waistcoat that had belonged to George Washington. Even after these sales, his collection still filled his various residences.

Unwanted Notoriety

In 1940, Orson Welles was best known for his work in radio, but that year George Schaefer offered him a contract to make two movies for RKO Radio Pictures. In fact, the deal was unusually generous, considering that Welles had never worked on a movie, let alone direct a film. The studio gave him complete control of the picture, from selecting the script to casting it, and most significant of all, signing off on the final cut. According to Welles, without the control the contract with RKO offered him, "I would never have made *Citizen Kane*. That's why I got that contract with Final Cut. Because George Schaefer didn't know any better! None of the other guys would have given me a contract like that."

Welles in 1941

With this contract in hand, Welles packed himself and most of the other members of the Mercury Theater troupe off to Hollywood and began planning for his first big picture, based on the short story *Heart of Darkness* by Joseph Conrad. He laid out all his plans for the film, only to have RKO veto it because it would be too expensive to make. They also nixed *The Smiler with the Knife* because they did not feel that Welles' choice of Lucille Ball for the lead was a good idea.

As is often the case, the third time was the charm. RKO agreed to have Welles make *Citizen Kane*, and Welles co-wrote the script with Herman J Mankiewicz, a writer for the former Mercury Theater (which was now known as The Campbell Playhouse after Campbell's sponsored it). In *The Making of Citizen Kane*, author Robert Carringer noted, "Welles's first step toward the realization of Citizen Kane was to seek the assistance of a screenwriting professional. Fortunately, help was near at hand. . . . When Welles moved to Hollywood, it happened that a veteran screenwriter, Herman Mankiewicz, was recuperating from an automobile accident and between jobs ... Mankiewicz was an expatriate from Broadway who had been writing for films for almost fifteen years."

Welles would go on to produce, direct and star in the film, which was loosely based on the life of newspaper magnet William Randolph Hearst but hinted at Hearst's own life enough that the newspaper magnate famously banned all mention of the movie in his newspapers. Though Welles was criticized for his unkind treatment of the lead female character, which was also based in part on Hearst's mistress, Marion Davies, the fault for that particular piece of film history lies with Mankiewicz. He had once been close friends with Davies and gathered much of his background for the film from her gossip about her life with Hearst, but the two had a falling out, and Mankiewicz chose to take out his anger in how he portrayed the Davies character in the film.

Mankiewicz

While people often associate *Citizen Kane* with Hearst, Welles also based the character on the newspaper publisher and founder of the famous literary prize, Joseph Pulitzer, as well as the mysterious millionaire recluse Howard Hughes. He was also influenced in his writing by Conrad's *Heart of Darkness*. In reference to being asked about the people who influenced the character of Kane, Welles explained, "I'd been nursing an old notion – the idea of telling the same thing several times – and showing exactly the same thing from wholly different points of view. Basically, the idea Rashomon used later on. Mank liked it, so we started searching for the man it was going to be about. Some big American figure – couldn't be a politician, because you'd have to pinpoint him. Howard Hughes was the first idea. But we got pretty quickly to the press lords." In addition to Hearst, Pulitzer, and Hughes, Welles was also inspired in his writing by his own life. For instance, Kane's early childhood is similar to Welles', including being turned over to a guardian. All in all, it's hard to say how many different figures from American history influenced the development of Charles Foster Kane.

Once Welles was finished with the script, he felt that it was a masterpiece worthy of the best technicians and actors that Hollywood had to offer. Rumor got around about what he was doing and people began to flock to him, wanting to be part of the picture. He had his choice of film crew, and he used it well. As far as the cast was concerned, he mostly picked people he had worked with in the Mercury Theater. He encouraged their input in the film, but he still moved at lightning speed, completing the shooting in just 10 weeks. Though he was a novice, Welles studied enough to quickly become an expert, and he explained how he went about directing *Kane*: "As it turned out, the first day I ever walked onto a set was my first day as a director. I'd learned whatever I knew in the projection room — from [John] Ford. After dinner every night for about a month, I'd run *Stagecoach*, often with some different technician or department head from the studio, and ask questions. 'How was this done?' 'Why was this done?' It was like going to school."

Even as the movie was still being worked on, rumors were swirling around the movie, and the twisted, almost incestuous family tree of Hollywood actors and actresses was shaking at every branch. For example, Mankiewicz gave a copy of the script to a friend of his, Charles Lederer, who was not only Marion Davies' nephew but was also now married to the former Virginia Welles. She was still angry at her ex-husband for his infidelity and was happy to have a chance to undermine his career. Hollywood gossip columnist Hedda Hopper heard the rumors and made it a point to attend the preview screening of the movie. She immediately reported back that the film was obviously based on Hearst's life, and he in turn began a battle to keep it from ever being shown. Not only did Hearst forbid his own media outlets from showing the film, but he also began to make calls to various people in Hollywood, sharing with them some of the secrets he knew about their lives that he had not published. Studio heads throughout the town were nervous, and they put together money to try to pay off RKO, offering them enough cash to get back every dime they had invested in the film if they would just surrender the negatives and prints to them. Having seen the film, and knowing its value, RKO refused and went ahead and released it at limited venues.

Although Hearst wasn't the only source for Kane, the depiction of Kane made clear how much damage could be done to Hearst's reputation, as one of his own biographers explained, "Welles' Kane is a cartoon-like caricature of a man who is hollowed out on the inside, forlorn, defeated, solitary because he cannot command the total obedience, loyalty, devotion, and love of those around him. Hearst, to the contrary, never regarded himself as a failure, never recognized defeat, never stopped loving Marion or his wife. He did not, at the end of his life, run away from the world to entomb himself in a vast, gloomy art-choked hermitage. Orson Welles may have been a great filmmaker, but he was neither a biographer nor a historian." Ironically, Welles claimed to cut something from the film that was a more explicit reference to Hearst, saying, "In the original script we had a scene based on a notorious thing Hearst had done, which I still cannot repeat for publication. And I cut it out because I thought it hurt the film and wasn't in keeping with Kane's character. If I'd kept it in, I would have had no trouble with Hearst. He wouldn't have dared admit it was him."

Hearst

Welles also tried to disassociate the character of Susan from Davies, which may have irked Hearst most of all: "That Susan was Kane's wife and Marion was Hearst's mistress is a difference more important than might be guessed in today's changed climate of opinion. The wife was a puppet and a prisoner; the mistress was never less than a princess. Hearst built more than one castle, and Marion was the hostess in all of them: they were pleasure domes indeed, and the Beautiful People of the day fought for invitations. Xanadu was a lonely fortress, and Susan was quite right to escape from it. The mistress was never one of Hearst's possessions: he was always her suitor, and she was the precious treasure of his heart for more than 30 years, until his last breath of life. Theirs is truly a love story. Love is not the subject of *Citizen Kane*."

As bad as his financial woes were, Hearst was so bitter about *Citizen Kane*, which was released on May 1, 1941, that even before its release, Hearst fought with all his money and power to prevent its release. He would go so far as to bring FBI Director J. Edgar Hoover into the fray. Journalist Jon Wiener explained, "The F.B.I. opened its file on Welles in 1941, just after the completion of his film Citizen Kane, when Hearst was using all the power he could command to block release of the thinly disguised biography of the antilabor publisher. (It has since been acclaimed as perhaps the greatest U.S. film.) …the Hearst press began describing Welles as a 'communist' at that point, first in a review of Welles's Broadway play *Native Son*…. Hearst's Journal American called it 'propaganda that seems closer to Moscow than Harlem.' The F.B.I. file contains forty-two pages on the play, including accusatory clips from Hearst papers. Two weeks later, when Welles's new radio series with the Free Company premiered--the group included such well-known subversives as poet Archibald MacLeish and fiction writer Sherwood Anderson, poet Stephen Vincent Benet and actor and musical writer George M. Cohan--the Hearst press called it 'communistic' and 'subversive.' A headline declared that Welles 'helps Reds.'…Hearst's critique of Welles's politics occupies a prominent place in the F.B.I. file. Citizen Kane is described there as 'inspired by [Welles's] close associations with communists over a period of years' and as 'nothing more than an extension of the Communist Party's campaign to smear one of its most effective and consistent opponents in the United States.' The file declares that 'the most intensive and extensive campaign which the Communist Party has conducted throughout its entire history has been its anti-Hearst campaign.'"

While Hearst was able to prevent many theaters in the nation from showing the movie, he could not keep critics away, and they wrote raving reviews that were lapped up by the public. *The New York Times* critic said the movie "comes close to being the most sensational film ever made in Hollywood" and continued, "Count on Mr. Welles: he doesn't do things by halves. ... Upon the screen he discovered an area large enough for his expansive whims to have free play. And the consequence is that he has made a picture of tremendous and overpowering scope, not in physical extent so much as in its rapid and graphic rotation of thoughts. Mr. Welles has put upon the screen a motion picture that really moves. As critic James Agate noted in his review, "*Citizen Kane* has entirely ousted the war as conversation fodder. Waiters ask me what I think of it, and the post is full of it. ... You know now that all the vulgar beef, beer and tobacco barons are vulgar because when they were about seven years of age somebody came and took away their skates. That is one explanation of this alleged world-shaking masterpiece, *Citizen Kane*. Another point of view is that *Citizen Kane* is so great a masterpiece that it doesn't need explaining. ... In the meantime I continue to steer a middle course. I regard Citizen Kane as a quite good film which tries to run the psychological essay in harness with your detective thriller, and doesn't quite succeed."

Gradually, one theater after another decided that they had more to lose by not showing *Citizen Kane* than by screening it. Although it's still critically acclaimed and widely recognized as one of Hollywood's greatest movies, the movie was not a financial success because too many theaters refused to show it, and those that did were often shocked by the results. *Citizen Kane* was too different from any other film at that time to be well accepted, and many people walked out in the middle of the movie, with some of them even asking for their money back. Welles later recalled, "For a couple of years after Kane, every time I walked in the streets in New York they shouted at me, 'Hey! What the hell is that movie of yours about? What does it mean?' Not, 'What is Rosebud?' but always 'what does it mean?'"

Regardless of the financial success, or lack thereof, the movie was nominated for nine Academy Awards, with Welles receiving four nominations for acting, writing, directing and producing the movie. Though he only won one of these, for Best Original Screenplay (an award shared with Mankiewicz), he was still thrilled with the film, even though RKO chose to put *Citizen Kane* in storage, perhaps in hopes that time would improve its popularity. The style in which the narrative progressed was clearly in line with Welles' opinion on what made a director good: "I want to give the audience a hint of a scene. No more than that. Give them too much and they won't contribute anything themselves. Give them just a suggestion and you get them working with you. That's what gives the theater meaning: when it becomes a social act."

Ultimately, RKO would not release it again until 1956, and by then, movies were seen more as an artistic medium than they had been in the early '40s. Young people, particularly the more sophisticated college students springing up on American campuses, flocked to see and talk about the film, and even today, it is still considered essential viewing for anyone interested in movie history. At the end of the 20th century, the American Film Institute named it the greatest movie Hollywood ever made.

While *Citizen Kane* was not literally autobiographical, it was philosophically autobiographical in that it reflected Welles' moral perspective on life, as noted by one of the more famous quotes in the movie: "The trouble is, you don't realize you're talking to two people. As Charles Foster Kane, who has 82,634 shares of Public Transit Preferred. You see, I do have a general idea of my holdings. I sympathize with you. Charles Foster Kane is a scoundrel. His paper should be run out of town. A committee should be formed to boycott him. You may, if you can form such a committee, put me down for a contribution of $1,000 dollars. On the other hand, I am the publisher of the Inquirer! As such, it's my duty - and I'll let you in on a little secret, it's also my pleasure - to see to it that decent, hard-working people in this community aren't robbed blind by a pack of money-mad pirates just because - they haven't anybody to look after their interests."

Though Hearst had no way of knowing it at the time, he might have been able to take grim satisfaction in the fact that *Citizen Kane* proved to be a millstone around Welles' neck, especially in time as it became clear that the novice director had already made the best movie of his life at the age of 26.

Hearst's Final Years

Like most of the United States, the Hearst Corporation began recovering from the Depression during World War II, and with Americans more interested than ever in daily news reports concerning the war, readership skyrocketed. At the same time, thanks to the mobilization brought about by the war, Americans had more disposable income and companies began spending more to advertise their goods to customers.

Hearst spent most of the war years at Wyntoon, and when the war was over, he returned to San Simeon and continued his building projects. He also returned to collecting art and antiques, though never again on the previous scale. As he grew older and came to grips with his own mortality, he began giving away many of his pieces, including donating some of them to the Los Angeles County Museum of Art.

With the war over but patriotism still at a fevered pitch, Hearst became particularly interested in promoting the stories of the nation in his publications. In 1945, he wrote to J. D. Gortatowsky, the president of King Features, concerning a new comic strip the company was developing: "I have had numerous suggestions for incorporating some American history of a vivid kind in the adventure strips of the comic section. The difficulty is to find something that will sufficiently interest the kids…. Perhaps a title 'Trained by Fate' would be general enough. Take Paul Revere and show him as a boy making as much of his boyhood life as possible, and culminate, of course, with his ride. Take Betsy Ross for a heroine, or Barbara Fritchie…for the girls."

His work on this project was among his last efforts. In 1947, he turned one last time to building, this time purchasing a mansion in Beverly Hills for $120,000. It sat on nearly 4 acres of land just three blocks from the famous Sunset Strip. To the Hearst family, it was known as the Beverly House. With three swimming pools, a nightclub, a movie theater on site, and tennis courts, the 29 bedroom home was, at one time, the most expensive private residence in the United States, with an estimated value of more than $165 million. Hearst lived the last three years of his life in that house, dying there on August 14, 1951. He was 88.

According to his obituary, published in the *Los Angeles Times*, "Mr. Hearst had been ill several years. Frequent reports of the serious condition of his health had caused concern throughout the Hearst domain. But the Chief, as he was known to the 27,000 workers of the various Hearst enterprises, rallied repeatedly to resume his active role as editorial head of his national chain of newspapers. Yesterday, however, he lapsed into a coma from which he did not awaken. Death came peacefully."

While all five of his sons were with him at his death, his wife Millicent had remained "at her home at Southampton, N.Y., where she was spending the summer. She said through a spokesman that she would leave for California last night for his funeral…Mr. Hearst's body was taken to the Pierce Bros. Beverly Hills Mortuary and later removed and flown to his native San Francisco.

There, it is understood, he is to be buried in Cypress Lawn Cemetery where his father, Sen. George Hearst, and his mother, Mrs. Phoebe Apperson Hearst, are buried. Funeral arrangements will be announced at a later date. The Los Angeles County Board of Supervisors and the City Council adjourned yesterday out of respect to the memory of Mr. Hearst. On orders of Mayor Bowron, the City Hall Flag was lowered to half staff."

Speaking on behalf of the city, Bowron said, "The people of our city have suffered a great loss. To hundreds of thousands of people in every walk of life, William Randolph Hearst was a great and true friend. … He was for a greater Southwest, a greater California, a greater Los Angeles. He was a constant and vigilant foe of corruption and deceit. We have lost a great crusader, a man who loved his country, a man who loved our city and its people."

In spite of his many moral lapses, Cardinal Francis Spellman said of the Catholic Hearst, "I mourn the death of a great American patriot…who fought battles on many fronts for all that America signifies and who leaves to posterity traditions to continue the fight for freedom and justice that will encourage and inspire Americans for many generations."

Finally, the president of the *United Press Associations* stated that "one of the great figures of journalism has gone from among us. But the newspaper empire he created lives as a memorial to his genius. William Randolph Hearst originated many of the forms of daily publishing which now are familiar to all, and introduced an era of intense competition which ever since has had a stimulating effect on the enterprise and ingenuity of newspapering. His life and career are a conspicuous part of the history of our times."

People in Hearst's lifetime had different takes on his life and career, and he continues to have a mixed legacy, but everyone can certainly agree that Hearst was conspicuous.

Online Resources

Other books about 19th century American history by Charles River Editors

Other books about 20th century American history by Charles River Editors

Other books about Hearst on Amazon

Other books about Pulitzer on Amazon

Further Reading

Brian, Denis. Pulitzer: A Life (2001) online edition

Carlson, Oliver (2007). Hearst – Lord of San Simeon. Read Books.

Davies, Marion (1975). The Times We Had: Life with William Randolph Hearst. Indianapolis:

Bobbs-Merrill.

Hearst, William Randolph, Jr. (1991). The Hearsts: Father and Son. Niwot, CO: Roberts Rinehart.

Ireland, Alleyne. Joseph Pulitzer: Reminiscences of a Secretary (1914)

Morris, James McGrath. Pulitzer: A Life in Politics, Print and Power (2010), a scholarly biography

Morris, James McGrath. "The Political Education of Joseph Pulitzer," Missouri Historical Review, Jan 2010, Vol. 104 Issue 2, pp 78–94

Nasaw, David (2000). The Chief: The Life of William Randolph Hearst. Boston: Houghton Mifflin

Pfaff, Daniel W. Joseph Pulitzer II and the Post-Dispatch (1991)

Procter, Ben H. (1998). William Randolph Hearst: The Early Years, 1863–1910. New York: Oxford University Press.

Procter, Ben H. (2007). William Randolph Hearst: The Later Years, 1911–1951. New York: Oxford University Press.

Rammelkamp, Julian S. Pulitzer's Post-Dispatch 1878–1883 (1967)

Swanberg, W.A. (1961). Citizen Hearst. New York: Scribner.

Swanberg. W.A. (1967). Pulitzer.

United States Congress. "Joseph Pulitzer (id: P000568)". Biographical Directory of the United States Congress. Retrieved on 2008-11-06

Whyte, Kenneth (2009). The Uncrowned King: The Sensational Rise of William Randolph Hearst. Berkeley: Counterpoint.

Free Books by Charles River Editors

We have brand new titles available for free most days of the week. To see which of our titles are currently free, click on this link.

Discounted Books by Charles River Editors

We have titles at a discount price of just 99 cents everyday. To see which of our titles are currently 99 cents, click on this link.

Printed in Great Britain
by Amazon